WRITERS AND THEIR WORK

ISOBEL ARMSTRONG
General Editor

T0313620

CHRISTOPHER SMART

CHRISTOPHER SMART

CHRISTOPHER SMART

Neil Curry

© Copyright 2005 by Neil Curry

First published in 2005 by Northcote House Publishers Ltd, Horndon, Tavistock, Devon, PL19 9NQ, United Kingdom.
Tel: +44 (01822) 810066. Fax: +44 (01822) 810034.

British Library Cataloguing-in-Publication Data
A catalogue record for this book is available from the British Library

ISBN 0-7463-1023-4 hardcover
ISBN 0-7463-1014-5 paperback

Typeset by TW Typesetting, Plymouth, Devon
Printed and bound by CPI Group (UK) Ltd, Croydon, CR0 4YY

For Kit, who didn't quite make it

Contents

Biographical Outline

1722	11 April: Christopher Smart born at Shipbourne, Kent.
1733	On death of father, family moves to Durham.
1734	Enters Pembroke College, Cambridge, as a sizar.
1742	Graduated BA.
1743	Awarded Fellowship of Pembroke College.
1747	Writes, produces, and acts in a comedy *The Grateful Fair, or, A Trip to Cambridge*. November: arrested for debt, but rescued by colleagues.
1749	Leaves Cambridge to live as a writer in London.
1750	'On the Eternity of the Supreme Being', his first success in the Seatonian Prize Competition at Cambridge. He also won the prize in 1751, 1752, 1753, and 1755.
1750–3	Edits and contributes to *The Student, or, the Oxford and Cambridge Miscellany* and *The Midwife, or, the Old Woman's Magazine*.
1751–2	Writes and performs in a revue, *The Old Woman's Oratory*, at The Haymarket Theatre. Evidence of a drinking problem.
1752	*Poems on Several Occasions*. Married Anna Maria Carnan, stepdaughter of his publisher, John Newbery. Moved to Canonbury House, Islington.
1753	*The Hilliad, an Epic Poem*. Daughter, Marianne ('Polly'), born.
1754	Daughter, Elizabeth ('Bess'), born.
1756	Suffers a serious illness. 'Hymn to the Supreme Being on Recovery from a Dangerous Fit of Illness'.

1757   March: application is made for his admission to St Luke's Hospital for the Insane. 'He insisted on people praying with him' (Johnson). Admitted in May.

1758   May: 'discharged uncured'. Admitted sometime before January 1759 to Mr Potter's Private Madhouse in Bethnal Green. Anna Maria Smart moves to Dublin and later to Reading, where she assumes managership of the *Reading Mercury*.

1763   January: Smart is released (rescued?) from the madhouse. April: *A Song to David*. November: *Poems on Several Occasions*.

1764   April: *Hannah, an Oratorio*, performed at the Haymarket Theatre.

1765   August: *A Translation of the Psalms of David*, which included *Hymns and Spiritual Songs for the Fasts and Festivals of the Church of England*.

1766   Threatened with arrest for debt.

1767   July: *The works of Horace. Translated into Verse*.

1768   *The Parables of Our Lord and Saviour Jesus Christ, Done into Familiar Verse. Abimelech, an Oratorio*, performed at the Haymarket Theatre.

1770   April: arrested for debt and imprisoned in the King's Bench Prison.

1771   *Hymns for the Amusement of Children*. 20 May: Smart dies in prison of 'a liver disorder'.

Abbreviations and References

All quotations from Christopher Smart's works are taken from *The Poetical Works of Christopher Smart*, ed. Marcus Walsh and Karina Williamson, 5 vols. (Oxford, 1980–96), abbreviated as *PW*. Where necessary, the abbeviation *JA* has been used for *Jubilate Agno*.

1

'Hymn to the Supreme Being' and the Seatonian Poems

How fashions change. In the 1960s the shock waves from a single line of Robert Lowell's 'Waking in the Blue' ('This is the house of the "mentally ill" ') reverberated around American and British poetry for more than a decade, doing much to establish his reputation, and giving rise to what became known as the 'Confessional School' of poetry, but when Christopher Smart pre-empted him by 200 years in his poem 'Hymn to the Supreme Being, On Recovery from a dangerous Fit of Illness' with the lines:

> When reason left me in the time of need,
> And sense was lost in terror or in trance,
>
> (ll. 21–2)

they did nothing at all to enhance *his* growing reputation; indeed they almost brought it to an end.

The 'Hymn to the Supreme Being' begins with a story from the Old Testament (Isa. 38), which Smart clearly intended to be understood as a parallel to his own story. It tells how Hezekiah, King of Israel, falls sick and is told by Isaiah that he is about to die. Hezekiah turns his face to the wall and remonstrates with God: has he not always kept the faith; has he not always lived a sinless life? God listens to the King's prayer, relents, and sends Isaiah back to announce that He will grant him an added fifteen years of life. This is one fact Smart omits from the story, ironically, so it turned out, as he himself had only another fifteen years to live after his own recovery.

1

Smart leaves the Old Testament story at this point and the poem enters a completely personal phase. Hezekiah had been able to look back upon a blameless life, but for Smart it is as though, like Noah, he had sent a raven flying off into his past to search out his good deeds, but it had found nothing whatsoever to bring back.

> I sent back memory, in heedful guise,
>   To search the records of preceding years;
> Home, like the raven to the ark, she flies,
>   Croaking bad tidings to my trembling ears.

(ll. 25–8)

However, all is not lost. There is still the dove, and the language of the Old Testament is now superseded by that of the New, as the dove comes down to us, bringing, like the New Testament itself, the Peace of God through redemption and forgiveness. At the hour of our death we are in 'Christ's own care', and it is through Christ that Smart is saved. He recovers his health, and his return to the bosom of his family is described in lines that, for their time, have a startling autobiographical frankness to them, but a frankness combined with such sentimentality that it makes for rather uncomfortable reading. We feel almost intrusive.

> The virtuous partner of my nuptial bands,
>   Appear'd a widow to my frantic sight;
> My little prattlers lifting up their hands,
>   Beckon me back to them, to life, and light;
> I come, ye spotless sweets! I come again,
> Nor have your tears been shed, nor have ye knelt in vain.

(ll. 49–54)

The poem is only at its halfway stage though, and what had begun as a historical narrative, then moved through a theological statement into autobiography, now gathers strength and demonstrates a power and virtuosity that Smart's poetry has not had before. There is a tightening of the structure within the grace of the lyric and this comes about, in part, through the device of *sequencing* that was to become such a feature of the later *A Song to David* (1763).

2

In stanza 11 of the 'Hymn to the Supreme Being' he lists some of the miraculous cures Christ had performed.

> He rais'd the lame, the lepers he made whole,
>   He fix'd the palsied nerves of weak decay,
> He drove out Satan from the tortur'd soul,
>   And to the blind gave or restor'd the day ...
>
> (ll. 61–4)

The feet, the nerves, the soul or mind, and the eyes: these become themes to be reworked in the next two stanzas. First he looks back into his own past when he was sick and could not walk and could not see, when his body shook and his mind seemed lost.

> My feeble feet refus'd my body's weight,
>   Nor wou'd my eyes admit the glorious light,
> My nerves convuls'd shook fearful of their fate,
>   My mind lay open to the powers of night.
>
> (ll. 67–70)

But he was saved and born again through Christ.

> He pitying did a second birth bestow
> A birth of joy – not like the first of tears and woe.
>
> (ll. 71–2)

Smart, therefore, dedicates his feet, his nerves, his eyes, and his soul to the service of his Saviour.

> Ye strengthen'd feet, forth to his altar move;
>   Quicken, ye new-strung nerves, th'enraptur'd lyre;
> Ye heav'n-directed eyes, o'erflow with love;
>   Glow, glow, my soul, with pure seraphic fire;
> Deeds, thoughts, and words no more his mandates break,
> But to his endless glory work, conceive, and speak.
>
> (ll. 73–8)

The poem then takes another change of direction. The story of Hezekiah is forgotten and so too is any thought of sickness, as Smart runs through a list (another characteristic of much of his later work) of minerals, elements, gems, flowers, birds, beasts, fish, and stars, telling us which is the finest example of each: gold being the finest of minerals; the diamond the best

3

of gems; the rose the best of flowers, and so on, concluding
with the assertion that man is greater than all of these.

> Yet what are these to man, who bears the sway?
> For all was made for him – to serve and to obey.

> (ll. 95–6)

It will become a central tenet of Smart's belief that it is
therefore incumbent upon man, and especially poets, to praise
God on behalf of all His creation. It is an idea that may perhaps
be glimpsed towards the end of the Hezekiah story. Isaiah 38:
20 reads: 'The Lord was ready to save me: therefore we will
sing my songs to the stringed instruments all the days of our
life in the house of the Lord.'

The poem finishes with a pledge. 'Thus ...' begins the
penultimate stanza, as if to persuade us that there is a logical
coherence of thought here, which there is not; the coherence is
emotional and it ends with an emotional pledge. What he
pledges is his charity or love:

> Deep-rooted in my heart then let her grow,
>   That for the past the future may atone;
> That I may act what thou hast giv'n to know,
>   That I may live for THEE and THEE alone,
> And justify those sweetest words from heav'n,
> 'THAT HE SHALL LOVE THEE MOST
> TO WHOM THOU'ST MOST FORGIVEN.'

> (ll. 103–9)

There is one more irony hiding in these closing lines, referring
as they do to the parable of the two debtors (Luke 7: 41–3), as
it was in a debtors' jail that Smart himself was to die when his
fifteen wretched and magnificent years came to an end.

The 'Hymn to the Supreme Being' marks a turning point
both in Smart's life and in his poetry, but it is hard to be certain
what the exact cause of it was. Ostensibly the new resolve was
on account of his gratitude at recovering from that 'dangerous
Fit of Illness', but what *precisely* was the nature of his illness?
The poem is prefaced by a fulsome dedicatory letter to Dr
James, the inventor of the famous Fever Powder, which,
together with the grace of God, seems to have brought Smart
back from the brink of death. He writes:

4

> Having made a humble offering to Him, without whose blessing your skill, admirable as it is, would have been to no purpose, I think myself bound by all the ties of gratitude, to render my next acknowledgements to you, who under God, restored me to health from as violent and dangerous a disorder, as perhaps ever man survived.[1]

This sounds a touch extreme and we need to remind ourselves that the publisher of this poem, and Smart's father-in-law, John Newbery, had acquired exclusive rights to the distribution of these same Fever Powders. He was a shrewd business man, keenly aware of the power of advertising, and so it is not impossible that it was he, rather than Smart, who composed the letter.

It is clear from the poem that what Smart was suffering from was not simply 'a fever'. There are at least three specific references to his disturbed mental state.

> When reason left me in the time of need,
>   And sense was lost in terror or in trance . . .

(ll. 21-2)

> And exil'd reason takes her seat again –

(l. 46)

> My mind lay open to the powers of night.

(l. 70)

If it was any kind of fever, it would seem to have been what used to be called a brain fever.

What we do know for certain is that the poem was published in June 1756 and that nine months later, in March 1757, an application was made for him to be admitted to St Luke's Hospital for the Insane and that he was eventually admitted in May of that year.[2]

To judge from Smart's observation on his own behaviour in *Jubilate Agno* –

> For I have a greater compass both of mirth and melancholy than another.

(B 132)

– he looks to have been suffering from manic depression, and what we know of his lifestyle up to this point does nothing to suggest otherwise. In March 1747 Thomas Gray wrote –

5

unkindly but prophetically – to his friend Thomas Wharton about a play, *A Trip to Cambridge*, that Smart had written: 'he can't hear the Prologue without being ready to die with Laughter. he acts five Parts himself, & is only sorry, he can't do all the rest ... all this, you see, must come to a Jayl, or Bedlam, & that without any help, almost without Pity.'[3]

Then there was the extravagance and the debt. In November of the same year Gray again wrote to Wharton to tell him that Smart had been arrested for a debt to a London Tailor of £50, which had been outstanding for three years: 'the Fellows went round to make out a list of his debts, which amount in Cambridge to above £350.'[4] And there was the drink. We have it on the authority of Dr Johnson that 'he used for exercise to walk to the alehouse but he was *carried* back again'.[5] And there is the irresponsible and irrepressible bonhomie. We hear of his wife complaining that he would often invite 'company to dinner, when no means appeared of providing a meal for themselves'.[6]

It is all too easy to see what it must have been like for her: what fun he must have been to be with, and what hell to live with. But who was he really? This extravagant, drunken debtor was also Christopher Smart MA, Fellow of Pembroke College, Cambridge, winner of the Craven Scholarship, and holder of Praelectorships in both philosophy and rhetoric, a man who seems to have been equally at home and equally as skilled in translating Horace as he was performing a drag act in a show called *Mrs Midnight's Oratory*. And while he was writing and editing magazines such as *The Student* and *The Midwife* under pen names as unlikely as Zosimus Zephyr and Ebernezer Pentweazle, he was also writing his five winning entries for the Seatonian Prize at Cambridge.

But once he had recovered from his 'dangerous Fit of Illness', the two sides of this complex personality were sealed and all the manic activity was channelled into one direction. He seems to have taken quite literally St Paul's words to the Thessalonians, 'Pray without ceasing', and those words are still fixed in his mind in one of the last poems he ever wrote:

> Pray without ceasing (says the Saint)
> Nor ever in the spirit faint;

> With grace the bloom and faith the root,
> The pray'r shall bring eternal fruit.
>
> ('Prayer', in *Hymns for the Amusement
> of Children*, ll. 1–4)

Johnson took a characteristically balanced view of the affair. He told Boswell:

> My poor friend Smart shewed the disturbance of his mind, by falling upon his knees, and saying his prayers in the street, or in any other unusual place. Now although, rationally speaking, it is a greater madness not to pray at all, than to pray as Smart did, I am afraid there are so many who do not pray, that their understanding is not called into question.

Clearly he felt some sympathy for him as he added: 'I did not think he ought to be shut up. His infirmities were not noxious to society. He insisted on people praying with him; and I'd as lief pray with Kit Smart as anyone else.'[7]

In *Jubilate Agno* we read Smart's own confession:

> For I blessed God in St James's Park till I routed all the
> company.

and

> For the officers of the peace are at variance with me, and the
> watchman smites me with his staff.
>
> (B 89–90)

He had to be locked up; he wasn't funny any more.

The intensity of this religious obsession might have been new to Smart, but religion itself was not, as can be seen from the Seatonian poems, which he had written during the preceding five years.

On his death in 1741, Thomas Seaton, an Anglican divine and hymn writer, bequeathed the rents from his estate in Kislingbury, Northamptonshire, to the University of Cambridge, for ever, on condition that the money should be awarded annually as a prize for the best poem written in English on one of the Attributes of the Supreme Being. It was a prize that Smart was to win five times in six years, prompting him to refer to it after his third success as 'my Kislingbury estate'.[8]

The Poetical Essay, as each of his Seatonian poems was subtitled, was a recognized literary genre, and therefore one to be approached in a recognized literary style, usually the grand style of Miltonic blank verse. Blank verse in itself presented Smart with no problem, but he was no essayist. He was no Thomson or Cowper. He was certainly no Pope. He never was a poet with something new to say; he was more of a borrower. Reviewing his *Poems on Several Occasions* in 1752, the *Monthly Review* observed, 'If our poet is chargeable with any fault in his better pieces, it is the being too free with the beauties of all other *English* writers. He is the boldest borrower we shall meet with among the men of real genius.'[9] In the opening lines of his first Seatonian poem, 'On the Eternity of the Supreme Being', he is already echoing *Paradise Lost*, borrowing from the Psalms, and quoting directly from the Book of Job – early evidence of that ability to make simultaneous use of a variety of sources that is so characteristic of the later poetry, and of *A Song to David* in particular.

Considering that 'Eternity' was Smart's first attempt at a verse essay, it is a remarkably accomplished piece with a good deal of enthusiasm and energy about it. It is also remarkable in that it gives us our first glimpse of two of his most central beliefs: one was the necessity in man for 'prayer and praise', and the other was his contention that all created nature likewise praised and adored God continually by its very existence, and that this praise and adoration was an expression of its gratitude to God for the infinite goodness of His act of Creation. It was the poet's task, as Smart saw it, to give voice to mute nature's praise of God, and at the very height of his powers, in his hymn on 'The Presentation of Christ in the Temple', he writes:

> I speak for all – for them that fly,
>   And for the race that swim;
> For all that dwell in moist and dry,
> Beasts, reptiles, flow'rs and gems to vie
>   When gratitude begins her hymn.
>
> (ll. 41–5)

In the second of his Seatonian poems, 'On the Immensity of the Supreme Being', which was awarded the prize in 1752,

Smart took this theme as his starting point, urging us to listen to nature as it offers up its prayer of thanksgiving, a prayer to which he intends to add his own voice:

> List ye! how nature with ten thousand tongues
> Begins the grand thanksgiving, Hail, all hail,
> Ye tenants of the forest and the field!
> My fellow subjects of th'eternal King,
> I gladly join your Mattins, and with you
> Confess his presence, and report his praise.

(ll. 6–11)

It would seem here that Smart has slightly sidestepped the actual topic he was given. This sounds more like the omnipresence of God rather than His Immensity, but as we read these poems more closely we realize that, despite the implication of the word 'On' in each of their titles, Smart never attempts to define the precise nature of any of the divine attributes, or ever seeks to prove, for instance, the Omniscience or the Goodness of the Supreme Being. The kind of rational argument that that would have entailed was never his forte; instead he concentrates on the glories of the natural world in such a way that they evince the *presence* of these qualities all around us.

And here, with infectious delight, Smart takes us on an imaginative journey through the universe to witness for ourselves this glorious presence of God. First we are taken up into the 'spangled sky' to see the comets, the planets, and their satellites, then down onto 'Ocean's boist'rous back'. From the heights to the depths, we plunge beneath the waves, down to the 'pearl-pav'd bottom' of the sea, where little fish are swimming among coral gardens and shrubs of amber, and where the whale proudly surveys his domain. Further down, through the 'genial bowels of the earth', we go to see the precious stones and jewels deep under Pegu and Ceylon, then spring up 'Thro' beds of magnets, minerals and spar, Up to the mountain's summit', where we look down upon the smooth meadows and the trees of the forest. A linnet is singing. In the distance are towns and cities, but we realize now that these works of man are as nothing compared with the wonders we have seen. Man builds, but nothing to equal the ring-dove's

9

nest. He paints, but he cannot equal the blossom of the hawthorn or the cherry. Then, with the journey complete, Smart tells us that such evidence of God is unnecessary, for, even if these wonders did not exist, even if there were no birds, flowers, beasts, or gems, if there were only man, he would still know the glory of God, because God has His home within the body of man too. Therefore Smart will use his body – he will bend his knee, and his tongue will give praise.

> The knee, that thou hast shap'd, shall bend to Thee,
> The tongue, which thou hast tun'd, shall chant thy praise,
> And, thine own image, the immortal soul,
>   Shall consecrate herself to Thee for ever.

(ll. 142–5)

Condensing the poem in this way shows the smooth development of its theme. Of course it could be argued that Smart is doing little more than rehearse ideas put forward by men like John Ray and William Derham, the *physico-theologians*, as they are called, whose immensely popular works catalogued examples demonstrating 'the Being and Attributes of God from his Work of Creation', but, even if the ideas are commonplace, the expression of them is eloquent.

The *Monthly Review* was impressed. Its review, in the issue for May 1751, begins, 'Mr Smart has already gained so much reputation by several small pieces published in *The Student*, or otherwise, that it would be superfluous in us to say more of his character as a poet.' It adds later, 'Mr Smart has kept that most divine poet the *Psalmist* in his eye, almost throughout the whole of this work, and finely imitated him in several passages.'[10]

The poem is clearly the work of a maturing poet. The range of reference is itself impressive, and there is evidence of a growing skill and a more confident control over the verse form. The lines on the ring-dove show an ingenious blend of the ordinary and the audacious.

> the ring-dove's nest – on that tall beech
> Her pensile house the feather'd Artist builds –
> The rocking winds molest her not; for see,
> With such due poize the wond'rous fabrick's hung,

> That, like the compass in the bark, it keeps
> True to itself and steadfast ev'n in storms.
>
> (ll. 113–18)

The periphrases 'pensile house' and 'feather'd Artist' are standard, but they are coupled with genuine observation from nature and then brought to a close with a compass image as exact and almost as surprisingly metaphysical as that of John Donne himself.

The following year, 1752, may perhaps have been the most joyous Smart ever knew. There was his marriage to Anna Maria Carnan, and also the publication of his first full-length book, a handsome volume, *Poems on Several Occasions*. The notice it received from the *Monthly* was long and thorough, concluding, 'Enough will be seen in these and other specimens from the most finished of these pieces, to justify us in giving mr. *Smart* a place among the first of the present race of *English* poets.'[11]

Did success go to his head? His third Seatonian poem, 'On the Omniscience of the Supreme Being', he dedicated to the Archbishop of Canterbury. Confidently it goes off on a tangent again, and, after a brief glance at Omniscience, Smart is soon immersing himself in the workings of instinct, which he seems to regard as the operation of the wisdom of God in animals: magpies and jays never eat deadly nightshade; a sick dog knows what sort of grass will make it better; turkey chicks feign death to avoid the hawk. As vignettes they have some charm, but as exempla they are commonplace and cannot sustain the weight of Miltonic finery they are dressed up in. Pompous and verbose, his sentences strut or teeter along for anything up to a dozen lines, verging at times on the absurd.

For all its weaknesses, the poem does have moments of success, especially in the labyrinthine thought process whereby the nightingale's navigational instinct leads to Newton's failure to establish the longitude, and Newton's failure calls forth Solomon, whose command 'Go to the ant, thou sluggard' prompts a long and dramatic description of the sage industrious ant struggling back to its nest with a corn seed, and all this ending up with the remarkable piece of information that when she gets it there she

11

>   nips
> With subtle tooth the grain, lest from her garner
> In mischievous fertility it steal,
> And back to day-light vegetate its way.

(ll. 137–40)

We do not know what the strength of the opposition was like in 1752, but he won the prize for a third time, and again in 1753 with 'On the Power of the Supreme Being'.

Uncharacteristically, what Smart gives us in this poem is an account of the *destructive* power of God. When He speaks, it is not with the creative power of the Word; His voice brings about instead thunder and earthquake, whirlwinds and hurricanes. It is an unusually loud poem.

> Wherefore, ye objects terrible and great,
> Ye thunders, earthquakes, and ye fire-fraught wombs
> Of fell Volcanos, whirlwinds, hurricanes,
> And boiling billows hail! in chorus join
> To celebrate and magnify your Maker.

(ll. 73–7)

God shows His power by drowning the Egyptians in the Red Sea and helping Samson to slaughter the Philistines. This is Jehovah, the terrifying god of the Old Testament, whose violence Smart was to eradicate totally from his version of the Psalms. These Old Testament barbarities are so foreign to Smart's later view of God that we would hardly recognize the poem as being his at all were it not for its closing moments, where he turns to the love and mercy of God. Smart won the prize again, and the *Monthly Review* recorded the fact, but made no comment, a rather charitable restraint on their part, as there is a good deal that could be said against this poem, yet its failings do provide a useful pointer to where the strengths of Smart's poetry were to lie.

The scale of *Paradise Lost* is partly what gives Milton's verse its grandeur, but it is precisely here that Smart's verse fails. He cannot operate on a vast scale. *A Song to David* is a long poem, but its length is not due to a sustained and continuous progression; instead, as will be seen, Smart uses the rhetorical device of statement and amplification. For example, in stanza 4 of the *Song* he enumerates the twelve virtues of David and

12

then devotes one complete stanza to each of those virtues separately. Smart is not an expansive poet. He is at his best when he can work through individual stanzas – or units, as in *Jubilate Agno*. He translated the Psalms in this way: one stanza to one verse. He is too much of a miniaturist to deal successfully with the vastness of such a subject as the *Power* of God, unless it can be broken down into small pieces. This is what he did in 'Omniscience', but in this fourth poem he makes a bid for the grand Miltonic sweep and fails because he is denying himself the opportunity for the kind of precision he was good at.

It was five years now since Smart had been in residence at Pembroke College, and in 1753 the discovery of his marriage had finally forced the authorities to revoke his scholarship, but whatever they thought of his *Mother Midnight* escapades in London, they still regarded his successes in the Seatonian Prize as bringing honour to the College and in January 1754 it was declared that Mr Smart should 'have leave to keep his name in the College books without any expense, so long as he continue to write for the premium left by Mr Seaton'.[12]

This, ironically, was the year when Smart did not enter the competition, as the *Gentleman's Magazine* expressly noted.[13] There is no way of knowing why he did not, but an answer might lie in a poem published in that magazine in the same year, 'Ode to a Virginia Nightingale'. There is an explanatory note under the title, which reads, 'which was cured of a Fit in the bosom of a young Lady, who afterwards nursed the Author in a dangerous illness'.

As we have seen, he used almost the same words in his 'Hymn to the Supreme Being' and in his prefatory letter to Dr James he had written, 'This was the third time that your judgment and medicine rescued me from the grave.' It may be assumed, therefore, that this illness of 1754 was both dangerous and also of the mind. However, it had no effect on his final Seatonian poem, 'On the Goodness of the Supreme Being', which, we are told, he finished only just in time to send it to Cambridge to be judged.[14]

It is the most sensuous and the most luxuriant of all his Seatonian poems and the nearest in tone to *A Song to David*. Smart's growing preoccupation with David is evident from the first line, which puts forward the curious notion that King David and Orpheus are the same person.

> ORPHEUS, for so the Gentiles call'd thy name,
> Israel's sweet Psalmist, who alone couldst wake
> Th' inanimate to motion; who alone
> The joyful hillocks, the applauding rocks,
> And floods with musical persuasion drew;
> Thou who to hail and snow gav'st voice and sound,
> And mad'st the mute melodious!
>
> (ll. 1–7)

Smart makes this his own aim: to wake the inanimate to motion and to make the mute melodious. This is to be a Benedicite and his mind ranges over all the things on which the 'thought-kindling light' of God has ever fallen: the birds and the animals, the morning dew, garnets, lilies, tulips, auriculae, the peacock and the pansy, nectarines, dock and hemlock, blackbirds, thrushes, wooklark, redbreasts and ravens. Then indoors to the stained-glass windows of a cathedral, which brings to mind the sound of its organ and the singing of the choir.

> O He is good, he is immensely good!
> Who all things form'd, and form'd them all for man . . .
>
> (ll. 81–2)

On this basis there is nothing he need exclude; he can go on adding to these sparkling miniatures as long as the fancy takes him. A new order is established with the introduction of a pageant in which he envisages Asia, Arabia, Africa, India, and finally the whole of Christian Europe all coming to offer their thanks to God, and each bringing their own particular form of tribute. The elephants of Asia have 'tow'r-crown'd backs' and carry 'turban'd tyrants'. Arabia brings cassia, frankincense, and myrrh. The Africans, with painted plumes, and bows and arrows, have camels laden with ingots of gold, and the Indian comes in his 'brilliant crown and vest of furr' bearing pomegranates and 'the rich ananas'.

It is all deliciously exotic; a poem of such happiness and splendour – qualities that at this time were fast disappearing from Smart's own life. Even the *Monthly Review*, which had been so supportive, treated him only to a shower of petty sarcasms this time, amongst which we find the astonishing piece of news that 'elephants cannot kneel'.[15]

This was the last poem with which Smart won the Seatonian Prize. Another 'dangerous fit of illness' occurred and within a year and a half he had been admitted to St Luke's Hospital for the Insane. Coming between these two events, the 'Hymn to the Supreme Being' can be seen to mark a turning point in both his life and his poetry. In its closing lines he pledged himself to God, but midway, in a stanza that seems to distinguish and separate the abstract from the personal, Jehovah from Christ, the old from the new, he lists and names his own Seatonian poems:

> All glory to th' ETERNAL, to th' IMMENSE,
>   All glory to th' OMNISCIENT and GOOD,
> Whose power's uncircumscrib'd, whose love's intense;
>   But yet whose justice ne'er could be withstood,
> Except thro' him – thro' him, who stands alone,
> Of worth, of weight allow'd for all Mankind t' atone!
>
> (ll. 55–60)

It is as though he is bidding farewell to them. They are now part of his past. There will be no more attempts to deal with abstract topics in an aloof, impersonal tone. Here Smart is writing in the first person, and about his own life and problems and with an unprecedented frankness. There will be no more blank verse either. He has adopted the tightly organized Spenserian stanza and is instantly at home in it. He is a lyric poet. His lines rhyme.

He had found a new poetic voice and he had found a new self. To abandon the accepted and safe conventions of poetry, profitable though they had been for him, was one thing, but that other innovation, when put into practice, disturbed people so much that they had him shut away.

Of course one feels sorry for the man, but locking him up could be regarded as having been the making of him as a poet: no drink, no debts, no need to scribble for money. He had never before had the freedom to write the kind of poetry of which he was capable. Confinement gave him that freedom and allowed him to produce his finest work, but when he was

15

eventually released no one wanted to know about it. Gray actually thought he was dead,[16] and the *Monthly Review* quickly killed him off as a poet with a few lines on *A Song to David*, which were to become famous.

> It would be cruel, however, to insist on the slight defects and singularities of this piece for many reasons; and more especially if it be true, as we are informed, that it was written when the Author was denied the use of pen, ink and paper, and was obliged to indent his lines with the end of a key, upon the wainscot.[17]

2

Jubilate Agno

In a poem on Christopher Smart in his 1887 sequence *Parleyings with Certain People of Importance in their Day*, Browning eagerly accepted the wainscot and the key story, and he would not have been alone among nineteenth-century readers to do so. It chimed so well with the romantic view then current of the fate of genius: misunderstanding, persecution, and failure. However, the discovery of the manuscript of *Jubilate Agno* and its publication in 1939 proved that Smart had access to an ample supply of writing material, but it was a poem so unlike anything that had been seen before that at the outset it only intensified the belief that its author was a madman, and its first editor, W. F. Stead, set the tone by giving it the unfortunate subtitle: *A Song from Bedlam*.

From dates within the text, and from our knowledge of the methodical way in which Smart worked at his poem, adding to it day by day, it has been possible to establish that he began writing it at the very earliest in June 1758.[1] This means that none of it was written while he was confined in St Luke's Hospital for the Insane, as he was discharged from there as 'uncured' in May 1758. The next positive date we have is January 1759, by which time he is known to have been in a private madhouse run by Dr Potter in Bethnal Green, where he stayed until January 1763, and the last line of *Jubilate Agno* – it stops part way down the page – can be dated as having been written on 30 January of that year. So it was in a private madhouse, and *not* in Bedlam, that the poem was written, and it was ill advised of Stead to use that name with its Hogarthian connotations of degradation, brutality, and horror.

17

Much of the evidence points to a far more benign regime. Smart certainly had a garden. Johnson told Charles Burney that '[he] has partly as much exercise as he used to have; for he digs in the garden'.[2] And early in October 1762 Smart was expressing concern about it: 'the Lord succeed my pink borders' (D 118).

He must also have had a small library. This is clear from the wide range of reference in *Jubilate Agno*: no one could carry that amount of abstruse information in his head. Nor must it be forgotten that, as well as a garden, fresh air, exercise, and books, he had with him the most famous cat in the whole history of English literature – *Jeoffry*!

He was denied his freedom and held to be a madman, yet in some respects it was not a totally uncivilized existence, and it was certainly conducive to work. Within months of his release he had published *A Song to David*, and was issuing proposals for a subscription edition of his *Psalms* and *Hymns and Spiritual Songs*. There is, however, no mention of *Jubilate Agno* in his lifetime, and, whatever his original intentions were, it is improbable that he ever meant it for publication. What happened to the manuscript after he wrote that last line – which does not read like a *final* line – perhaps on the very day of his release, we cannot know. It may have been left behind. We do know that it came into the hands of the Revd. Thomas Cawardine, who was involved in the treatment of that other great eighteenth-century poet to be locked away for mental disorder, William Cowper. Cowper's confinement had begun shortly after Smart's release and Cawardine appears to have seen it as 'a kind of case study in poetic mania'.[3] What use to him it can have been is hard to imagine, but when he had finished with it the manuscript remained among his family papers until its significance was recognized by William Force Stead.

One of the peculiarities of the manuscript of *Jubilate Agno* is that the 'Let' and 'For' sections were written on separate sheets of paper, and that is how Stead published them. For all his brilliant and invaluable work on the text of the poem, he did not realize –with hindsight it is easy to be astonished by this – that the two parts were related to each other. It was not until 1954 that W. H. Bond, the Curator of Manuscripts at Harvard, eventually made the connection and showed that, to take a random example:

> Let Achsah rejoice with the Pigeon who is an antidote to malignity and will carry a letter.

should be followed by:

> For I bless God for the Postmaster general and all conveyancers of letters under his care especially Allen and Shelvock.

(B 22)

George Shelvocke (*sic*) was not only Secretary to the Postmaster General; he was also known to have an aviary of rare birds.

The method informing *Jubilate Agno*, these corresponding 'Let' and 'For' lines, can be seen to have had its origin in Robert Lowth's *Lectures on the Sacred Poetry of the Hebrews*, which Smart reviewed in the *Universal Visiter* in February 1756, calling it 'one of the best performances that has been published for a century'.[4] Lowth's was a truly important work, providing a major and lasting contribution to biblical studies, but where it touches chiefly on Smart is in what he says of the structure of Hebrew verse. Lowth established its dependence on what he called *parallelism*, by which he meant that in each line a statement was made and then responded to in some way. This aspect of the verse, he suggested, was shaped by the nature of Hebrew religious ceremony: 'the sacred hymns were alternately sung by opposite choirs, and that one choir usually performed the hymn itself, while the other sung a particular distich . . .'.[5]

Within this antiphonal structure he found three variations in the kinds of response which were made: 'namely, the amplification of the same ideas, the accumulation of others, and the opposition or antithesis of such as are contrary to each other . . .'.[6] Instances of this same approach can be found throughout Fragment B of *Jubilate Agno*, where the 'Let' and 'For' verses are most closely linked.[7]

Lowth's exposition of Hebrew verse style does not however account for what can only be called the 'free verse' of *Jubilate Agno*, as he argued strongly that the Psalms are essentially metrical,[8] but Smart's 'free verse' clearly owes everything, as our ears tell us, to the distinctive rhythms of the Authorized Version.

19

Analysis of *how* Smart went about writing *Jubilate Agno* is not difficult; the difficult questions are those that ask *what* it was he was writing and *why*. To answer these one needs to look carefully at the opening of the poem, beginning with the title that Smart himself gave it: *Jubilate Agno*, 'Rejoice in the Lamb'.

Lambs are referred to frequently in the Bible, but, apart from the occasional metaphor in Isaiah, they are almost all literally *lambs*, and are being, or are about to be, sacrificed. The expression 'the Lamb of God', as a sacrificial image, which seems so central to Christian belief and terminology, is found nowhere except in the writings of St John. His is the only Gospel that uses this expression: 'The next day John seeth Jesus coming unto him, and saith, Behold the Lamb of God, which taketh away the sin of the world' (John 1: 29). In Revelation (7: 9–10) the image is fully developed, and this appears to have been Smart's starting point.

> 9. And after this I beheld, and, lo, a great multitude, which no man could number, of all nations, and kindreds, and people, and tongues, stood before the throne, and before the Lamb, clothed with white robes, and palms in their hands;
> 10. And cried with a loud voice, saying, Salvation to our God which sitteth upon the throne, and unto the Lamb.

And more importantly, in Revelation 5: 13:

> 13. And every creature which is in heaven, and on the earth, and under the earth, and such as are in the sea, and all that are in them, heard I saying, Blessing, and honour, and glory, and power, be unto him that sitteth upon the throne, and unto the Lamb for ever and ever.

Seen in this light the beginning of *Jubilate Agno* has a great beauty and great daring to it.

> Rejoice in God, O ye Tongues; give the glory to the Lord, and the Lamb.
> Nations, and languages, and every Creature, in which is the breath of Life.
> Let man and beast appear before him, and magnify his name together.
>
> (A 1–3)

What is happening here is that the reader has become a witness before the throne of God, as a man and a creature step forward together to praise and magnify the Lord and the Lamb. With the exception of man, creation is mute; the creatures may make sounds, but they have no words, so it is incumbent upon man to speak for and on behalf of creation. Each man has chosen to come forward with a creature he can identify with, or relate to, and so speak for.

The first to step forward are, quite properly, the Patriarchs, but Smart never allows the Old Testament to be disassociated from the New, and at the outset the many-faceted nature of his thinking is present in the association of Noah's Ark with the Ark of Salvation, a conjunction of ideas that is there in the Baptismal Service when a child is 'received into the Ark of Christ's Church'.

> Let Noah and his company approach the throne of Grace, and do homage to the Ark of their Salvation.
>
> (A 4)

For the most part the connections between the man and the beast are clear. Abraham steps forward with a ram (Gen. 22), Balaam with an ass (Numb. 22), and Daniel with a lion (Dan. 6), and when they are less clear the Bible provides the source.

> Let Isaac, the Bridegroom, kneel with his Camels, and bless the hope of his pilgrimage.
>
> (A 6)

In Genesis 24, Rebekah was recognized as being Isaac's future bride when she offered to draw water from the well for the kneeling camels.

After the patriarchs come the priests (A 15–24), but Smart, an animal lover,[9] will not have them *sacrifice* their animals; they *sanctify* them and let them go free.

> Let Aaron the high priest, sanctify a Bull, and let him go free to the Lord and Giver of Life.
>
> (A 15)

He also has these priests present themselves in the company of beasts that, according to Deuteronomy, were 'unclean': the chamois, the pygarg, the coney, and the hare. Evidently he believed, as did Blake, that everything that lives is holy.

Following the patriarchs and the priests come the politicians and military leaders, and the deliverers of Israel (A 25–32), Moses, Joshua, and Gideon, but after them, although the references continue to be apposite, there is no discernible order. The names simply continue; the procession seems endless.

One line without a specific name in it –

> Let A Little Child with a Serpent bless Him, who ordaineth strength in babes to the confusion of the Adversary.

> (A 90)

– comes at the end of the list of animals and recalls the verse in Isaiah 11: 6 where 'The wolf also shall dwell with the lamb ... and a little child shall lead them.' As a child, Heracles strangled two serpents in his cradle, but here he blesses them, and it is the strength of the Christ Child, clearly alluded to in both references, that will defeat Satan, the Adversary.

After the beasts come the insects – the silkworm, the butterfly, the bee, and so on – and bookish references begin to be replaced by natural observation.

> Let Anaiah bless with the Dragon-fly, who sails over the pond by the wood-side and feedeth on the cressies.

> (A 100)

It ends with a sequence of seven birds, where Smart's lyricism is at last allowed to be heard.

> Let Benjamin bless and rejoice with the Redbird, who is soft and soothing.
> Let Dan rejoice with the Blackbird, who praises God with all his heart, and biddeth be of good cheer.

> (A 112–13)

But were we to stop at the end of Fragment A and ask where all this has got us, the answer would have to be: *not very far*. The initial conception, sublime as it was, was always too static to allow of any forward progression. Once all these men and all these creatures had presented themselves before the Throne of the Lamb, what were they to do? They have, it can be assumed, entered into eternity, but at the outset of his Seatonian poem on that theme Smart had admitted that eternity was 'INCOMPREHENSIBLE'.

With the beginning of Fragment B, however, a new dimension is added to the poem. We now have the 'For' verses, and in the first of them is the word 'I'. With so few letters, and without any form of journal, this is our only source of personal statement, and it is therefore invaluable to our understanding of Smart's way of thinking and feeling.

In the first 150 lines of these 'For' verses he looks back over his life: to the Fairlawn estate at Shipbourne in Kent where he was born, the 'meadows, the brooks and the hills' (B 119); to Cambridge (B 69); to his becoming a Freemason (B 109); to Canonbury House in Islington (B 75), where he lived after his marriage and where his children were born. He prays for all fatherless children, though they are 'never deserted of the Lord' (B 70). He thinks back to the commotion he caused in St James's Park where he prayed so vehemently that he 'routed all the company' (B 89) and felt the force of the watchman's staff. He knew what the trouble was: 'For I have a greater compass both of mirth and melancholy than another' (B 132). And now, as a result, he is in 'jeopardy', as he calls it (B 1). He does seem to have been treated very harshly at the start. He may have been kept in a dark cell (B 147). He was physically abused with 'harping-irons' (B 124). Some people did not expect him to live through it. 'They lay wagers touching my life,' he writes, adding ruefully, 'God be gracious to the winners' (B 92). He prays for all those locked up with him, 'all my brethren and sisters in these houses' (B 123). He is taunted, 'For silly fellow! silly fellow! is against me and belongeth neither to me nor my family' (B 60). He feels humiliated by being such a spectacle (B 63), but, for all that has happened to him, he cannot and would not change it. 'For I am under the same accusation with my Saviour – for they said, he is besides himself' (B 151) and he would die for Him. 'For I am ready to die for his sake – who lay down his life for all mankind' (B 98).

In one of the most curious and beautiful lines in the whole poem he seems to accept his lot. 'For in my nature I quested for beauty, but God, God hath sent me to sea for pearls' (B 30). His lot is to sing (B 32). He will write poems to the glory of

God, and he prays for his writing, 'For I pray the Lord Jesus to translate my MAGNIFICAT into verse and represent it' (B 43). He seems hopeful of ultimate success (B 3) and even freedom, 'For I have translated in the charity, which makes things better and I shall be translated myself at the last' (B 11), even if it is only in heaven.

And this is only to read vertically down the 'For' verses. In the 'Let' verses the men and the creatures have kept on coming. The links that are now established between the two sets of verses are often perfectly logical.

> Let Sarah rejoice with the Redwing, whose harvest is in the frost and snow.
> For the hour of my felicity, like the womb of Sarah, shall come at the latter end.

> (B 16)

The redwing is a winter migrant to Britain and so its food supply is a late harvest, as was the birth of a child to Sarah (Gen. 17: 17), and Smart too looks for a happy ending to his plight.

Or, even more clearly:

> Let James rejoice with the Skuttle-Fish, who foils his foe by the effusion of his ink.
> For the blessing of God hath been on my epistles, which I have written for the benefit of others.

> (B 125)

While some are puns:

> Let John, the Baptist, rejoice with the Salmon – blessed be the name of the Lord Jesus for infant Baptism.
> For I am safe, as to my head, from the female dancer and her admirers.

> (B 140)

with its play on Salmon/Salome.

Fish make their appearance when Smart changes at B 123 from Old to New Testament names, and begins with the apostles, who were fishers of men, and firstly with those who were actually fishermen.

24

LET PETER rejoice with the MOON FISH who keeps up the life in the waters by night.

FOR I pray the Lord JESUS that cured the LUNATICK to be merciful to all my brethren and sisters in these houses.

(B 123)

We have seen how Smart was feeling, and at B 157 we begin to see evidence of his way of thinking. Some large claims have been made for the quality of Smart's thinking, especially in relation to scientific matters.[10] It is true that while he was at Cambridge the sciences were in the ascendant and there is a great deal of reference to scientific matters in Section B, but Karina Williamson is right when she says that Smart's mind is 'fundamentally unscientific'.[11] It is not merely that he includes in his lists creatures as fantastical as the Leucrocuta, which is supposed to be part stag, part lion, and part badger. Fantasy is permissible in poetry, but when it comes to a serious intellectual challenge of the time, the squaring of the circle, and we find that Smart's answer is 'the Circle may be SQUARED by swelling and flattening' (B 374), we have to realize that this is a joke and was meant to be a joke. This must make us careful; Smart did warn us 'for I shou'd have avail'd myself of waggery . . .' (B 17).

There was no trace of waggery in 1752 when he was writing his Seatonian Poem 'On the Omniscience of the Supreme Being' and he described Sir Isaac Newton as 'Illustrious name, irrefragable proof / Of man's vast genius, and the soaring soul!' (ll. 92–3), but in the intervening six years his views changed and Newton seems to have become as much a villain for Smart as he was for Blake. He goes on the attack:

For Newton nevertheless is more of error than of the truth, but I am of the WORD of GOD.

(B 195)

And again:

Newton is ignorant for if a man consult not the WORD how should he understand the WORK?

(B 220)

The dichotomy between the Word of God and the Works of God's creation is at the root of the argument. The science of the

25

time was empirical; it looked at the material world and constructed general theories from analyses of particular instances. It did not seek to understand the particular by relating it to the whole as it was revealed to us through the word of God. It was empiricism versus revelation and this empirical, materialist philosophy was what Smart was rejecting: 'the philosophy of the times ev'n now is vain deceit' (B 219). This is an expression that he uses twice: at B 130 he again writes, 'For I am inquisitive in the Lord, and defend the philosophy of the scripture against vain conceit.' These words come from a warning St Paul issued in his epistle to the Colossians 2: 8: 'Beware lest any man spoil you through philosophy and vain deceit, after the tradition of men, after the rudiments of the world, and not after Christ.' 'Vain deceit' can be seen as a philosophy that favoured the rudiments of the world as opposed to the teachings of Christ, and Smart is rejecting what he regards as a resurgence of such attitudes in his own day.

His rejection is totally dogmatic. He sees no reason to argue his cause. He rejects without argument, and it is this that makes his thinking 'fundamentally unscientific'. He rejects Newton's calculation of the speed of light, 'For LIGHT is propagated at all distances in an instant because it is actuated by the divine conception' (B 284). The argument for the instant propagation of light simply being, we assume, Genesis 1: 3, 'And God said, Let there be light; and there was light.' Smart is well aware that Newton's calculations were based on observations of the eclipses of Jupiter's moons, but evidence such as that is of no significance to him. His next line reads: 'For the Satellites of the planet prove nothing in this matter but the glory of Almighty God' (B 285).

Likewise he rejected the accepted understanding of the barometer. 'For the rising in the BAROMETER is not effected by pressure but by sympathy' (B 213). He knows what the accepted understanding is, but rejects it, again without argument, in favour of the outdated, scholastic theory of sympathy. Smart was obviously an avid reader and we can see that he had a knowledge of the scientific developments of the time. From B 198 it is evident he knew of the Florentine Experiment, which had proved the incompressibility of water, but he counters it with 'For WATER is condensed by the Lord's FROST, tho' not by the FLORENTINE experiment.' It is almost flippant in its assertiveness, as is his assertion that 'the phenomenon of the horizontal moon is the truth – she appears bigger in the horizon because she actually is so' (B 426).

Newton's theory of colours is also rejected. 'For Newton's notion of colours is *alogos* unphilosophical' (B 648). He offers no reason for this other than that 'colours are spiritual' (B 649). In its place he substitutes his own colour circle: white, grey, blue, green, yellow, orange, red, black, purple, brown, pale, and back again to white (B 650–61). Rather arbitrary, particularly the move from red to black, but all he is prepared to say is that 'NOW that colour is spiritual appears inasmuch as the blessing of God upon all things descends in colour' (B 662).

That Smart had read Newton can be seen from lines B 160–4, where he deals with the first five principles of the *Principia*: matter, motion, resistance, and centripetal and centrifugal forces in that order. His comment on the last two is revealing. 'For the Centripetal and Centrifugal forces are GOD SUSTAINING and DIRECTING' (B 163). His world is God-centred, and God is *in* everything. His first Seatonian poem had begun:

> Hail, wond'rous Being, who in pow'r supreme
> Exists from everlasting, whose great Name
> Deep in the human heart, and every atom
> The Air, the Earth, or azure Main contains
> In undecipher'd characters is wrote –
>
> ('On the Eternity of the Supreme Being', ll. 1–5)

His objection to Newton's theory of colours is that it was *alogos* – literally without the word – and in B 195 he stated that, while Newton was in error, 'I am of the WORD of GOD.' The word is God's creative power. In Genesis God *speaks* the world into existence. This is the foundation of Smart's belief, together with the resonant verses at the start of John's Gospel: 'In the beginning was the Word.' What he objects to is the materialism of Newton's universe, and opposes it with his own claim, 'For nothing is so real as that which is spiritual' (B 258).

Newton believed in the physical properties of matter, and he believed that matter was inert, which again is something that Smart rejects out of hand. 'For I have shown the Vis Inertiae to be false, and such is all nonsense' (B 183). No argument. It is just nonsense. Matter is not inert. God lives in all of it. God is in the tides of the ocean (B 157), in every atom (B 160), in the loadstone (B 167), and in the thunder (B 272). 'For THUNDER is the voice of God direct in verse and musick.' God speaks and the earth replies, 'For EARTH which is an intelligence hath a voice and a propensity to speak in all her parts' (B 234)

In his first Seatonian poem he had called God the 'GREAT POET OF THE UNIVERSE' ('On the Eternity of the Supreme Being', l. 21). As a poet, God will, like David, be a harpist too, and when He plays, the universe, which He may be said to play into being, responds in awe. Smart tells us so in four lines of a haunting beauty:

> For GOD the father Almighty plays upon the HARP of stupendous magnitude and melody.
> For innumerable Angels fly out at every touch and his tune is a work of creation.
> For at that time malignity ceases and the devils themselves are at peace.
> For this time is perceptible to man by a remarkable stillness and serenity of soul.

> (B 246–9)

Once Smart had finished with these observations on science[12] and philosophy, it is as though he loses interest in it for a while, and the writing becomes very scrappy. W. H. Bond wrote in his Introduction to *Jubilate Agno* that the poem 'began as a genuine outpouring of poetical inspiration and ended as a device with little purpose beyond recording the passage of time, as mechanical as the notches on Crusoe's stick'.[13] There is something so appropriate about this image of futility in isolation. Smart does indeed now seem to begin scratching about for ways, especially sequences, that will allow him to fill the space and fulfil the daily task he had set himself.

The sequences he does try out have a mechanical feel to them. There is a list of genealogies that have little of interest though plenty of oddity. 'For the DUTCH are the children of Gog' (B 439). Another sequence is about the shape of the Hebrew letter *lamed*. There are two separate alphabetical sequences, only remarkable for their weak puns. 'For B is a creature busy and bustling' (B 514) and 'For H is not a letter,

but a spirit . . .' (B 520). There is a section on the musical value
of rhyme words. Then comes a sequence associating his own
system of twelve cardinal virtues with the twelve sons of Jacob
and connecting each with people of his own time. There is a
pun on 'the mouse (Mus)' being an essential part of the Latin
language because of 'Edi-mus, bibi-mus, vivi-mus' (B 637) and
a suggestion that the corresponding animal in English is the
Bull because it is there in such words as 'Invisible'. It is getting
nowhere, and then out of this nowhere we come to:

> For I will consider my Cat Jeoffry.
>
> (B 695)

In the scholarly editions of *Jubilate Agno* the footnotes come
to an almost complete stop here, just at the moment when this
poem, which has featured the drab, the eccentric, the elaborate,
the polished, the ornate, the brilliant, and the sophisticated,
suddenly becomes simple. They are lines that most people first
meet outside the context of the poem as a whole, as they are
probably the most anthologized *extract* in our literature. It is a
well-loved extract, yet one about which writers on Smart have
had little to say, but as these lines form by far the longest
continuous sequence in the poem there must be some reason
for them being there.

Before looking at what they say, it is worth while looking at
the way in which they work as poetry. 'For I will consider my
Cat Jeoffry.' That ten-syllable line surprises the ear with a
promise of regularity, but it is no pentameter and what follows
is an astonishing example of free verse where the variation of
rhythm and line length is what sings to us. Free verse in the
eighteenth century is odd enough, but what is odder still is
that some of the lines have a pattern to them that seems to echo
the Old English alliterative tradition.

> For at the first glance of the glory of God in the east he worships
> in his way.
>
> (B 697)

> For if he meets another cat he will kiss her in kindness.
>
> (B 714)

While others are paired in a truly Augustan balance.

> For there is nothing sweeter than his peace when at rest.
> For there is nothing brisker than his life when in motion.
>
> (B 738-9)

There is so much skill in evidence everywhere you look and *listen*.

> For he can jump from an eminence into his master's bosom.
>
> (B 749)

That tiny pause, which seems so inevitable after the word 'jump', perfectly re-creates the movement, the passage through the air.

Elsewhere a series of long vowel sounds enacts the way Jeoffry stretches out his paws:

> For thirdly he works it upon stretch with the fore paws extended.
>
> (B 705)

While the sounds in

> For he can tread to all the measures upon the musick.
>
> (B 766)

dance their way along the line.

Smart offers to *consider* his cat Jeoffry and the observation is keen, the description vivid, yet it is all performed with the utmost economy: hardly a noun that comes carrying along an adjective with it.

There is a simplicity, almost a naivety, to these lines. Readers cannot help but warm to this man telling us so unselfconsciously how he plays with his cat, how he strokes it, throws a cork up into the air for it to catch, and teaches it to jump over a stick, but it is a naivety that is achieved through a remarkable range of innovation, especially in its verbs.

> For he can spraggle upon waggle at the word of command.
>
> (B 748)

> For he camels his back to bear the first notion of business.
>
> (B 754)

> For his ears are so acute that they sting again.
>
> (B 758)

And there is drama too. Suddenly we hear:

Poor Jeoffry! poor Jeoffry! the rat has bit thy throat.

It is so unexpected, and we are so involved in what is happening that we are relieved to hear in the next line that he is better again (B 740–1).

Charming as these lines are, they also have a purpose. Smart had twice referred in *Jubilate Agno* to his own system of twelve cardinal virtues. They were referred to briefly at B 355–8, more elaborately in a list incorporating the sons of Jacob at B 601–13, and they were expounded on at length in *A Song to David*, where stanza 4 begins:

> Great, valiant, pious, good, and clean,
> Sublime, contemplative, serene,
> Strong, constant, pleasant, wise!

A close look at these lines reveals that Jeoffry represents in himself *all* these twelve virtues, which play such an important part in Smart's thinking.

Jeoffry is obviously *great*, as English cats are the best in Europe (B 731) and he is a Cherub Cat (B 723). He is *valiant*, as he survived his fight with the rat (B 741). As 'the servant of the Living God duly and daily serving him' (B 696), his *piety* is in no doubt, nor is his *goodness*, as even God 'tells him he's a good Cat.' (B 726) There are several lines devoted to his *cleanliness* (B 701–7). Everything about him is *sublime* and there is 'a divine spirit . . . about his body ' (B 742). In his 'morning orisons' (B 721) he is surely *contemplative*, for 'he knows that God is his Saviour' (B 737). His *serenity* is such that 'there is nothing sweeter than his peace when at rest' (B 738). And his *strength*? In *A Song to David* David's strength is shown in that he 'could defy Satan' and here each night Jeoffry 'counteracts the Devil' (B 720) with his glaring eyes. His *constancy*, his loyalty, are beyond question and he is 'tenacious of his point' (B 735). In the *pleasant* stanza of the *Song*, David is 'various as the year' and Jeoffry is blessed 'in the variety of his movements' (B 763). And, of course, he was *wise* enough 'to learn certain things' (B 744), such as jumping over a stick and catching a cork.

Jeoffry deserves seventy-four lines to himself, as it is clear that Smart regarded his companion as representing all possible virtues and therefore 'worthy to be presented before the throne of grace' (A 57), even though there are no cats in the Authorized Version of the Bible. As he had told us earlier, 'I am possessed of a cat, surpassing in beauty, from whom I take occasion to bless Almighty God' (B 68). It is no wonder that he thinks 'every house is incompleat without him and a blessing is lacking in the spirit' (B 728). A lover of puns himself, Smart would doubtless have agreed that Jeoffry was a Magnificat.

There is at least one missing folio at this point, depriving us of some nine months of Smart's regular entries, and Fragment C begins part way through another alphabetical sequence showing that God is in every letter, then one showing that he is in every number. Cleverly referring to the chainlike symbol for infinity, he shows that not only 'infinite upon infinite they make a chain' (C 37) but that the chain leads from man to God. 'For the last link is from man very nothing ascending to the first Christ the Lord of All' (C 38). However, although Smart is telling us of the links in this chain, there are no links apparent now between the 'Let' and the 'For' verses. The names are from the books of Ezra and Nehemia and the plants coupled with them are from eighteenth-century herbals, but even Smart seems to be losing interest in it:

Let Hanan rejoice with Poley of Crete.
For the mind of man cannot bear a tedious accumulation of nothings without effect.

(C 36)

He is not well. He was having trouble with his kidneys (C 50), suffering from catarrh and coughs and spitting blood (C 68–70). Nothing daunts his spirits though. Despite his situation, despite the humiliation he has suffered, his optimism never fails him, and when he starts a sequence of 'prophecies' there is no doom and gloom, 'For it is the business of a man gifted in the word to prophecy good' (C 57). It is Easter, the daffodils are out, and the glory of God has 'come down upon the trees' (C 60). All shall be well, and all manner of thing shall be well. No one is ever again going to get into his plight simply because he or she prayed in the streets, 'For I prophecy that the praise of God will be in every man's mouth in the Publick streets' and 'I prophecy that there will be Publick worship in the cross ways and fields (C 62–3). There will be 'great cheerfulness' everywhere (C 69). The clergy will set a better example (C 71). There will be mercy shown to criminals (C 65) and no one will be imprisoned for debt (C 72). Just how wrong he was about this he would find out for himself, and before very long.

There is also a slightly darker side to his thinking though. He looks forward to the downfall of the Roman Catholic Church (C 95) and expects there to be ' less mischief concerning women' (C 66), 'For I prophecy that they will be cooped up and kept under due control' (C 67).

There is an irrational side too. For over forty lines at the end of Fragment C Smart holds forth on the subject of *horns*. In the Vulgate, when Moses came down from Sinai, his face was said to be 'horned' (*cornuta esset*) from talking to God. Michelangelo's statue and other Renaissance representations of him show Moses with horns on his head. The words *shone* and *horn* have a common root in Hebrew and this seems to have been the cause of the story. The Authorized Version translated it as 'the skin of his face shone'. Smart accepts the Vulgate *literally*. All the Jews once had horns, according to him, and lost them only as a result of sinful intermarriage during the years of their captivity. We will grow our horns again though, he insists, and not metaphorically or symbolically. What is more, the English will 'recover their horns the first' (C 128). It is not easy to see how anyone could seriously suggest such a thing, but Smart was in poor health and Bond may be right when he says it is a 'sign of renewed mental disturbance'.[14] Much as one may admire Smart and his work, it would be foolish to assume that he was kept in Dr Potter's madhouse for all that time without there being, even if only intermittently, some cause for it.

If Dr Johnson felt that anyone trying to read Richardson for the story would hang himself, then it is hard to know what he would have found to say about *Jubilate Agno*. The grandeur with which it began has by the end degenerated into an almost robotic incantation of names and things. The things are mostly stones and herbs, and come from Pliny's *Natural History*. There is no personal experience or observation involved and the brief descriptions that accompany them frequently follow the exact wording of Ainsworth's Latin dictionary, even its errors. The names are no longer from the Bible, but are people of Smart's own day. Some he knew personally, but others have been shown to come from lists of births, deaths, and marriages, and appointments recorded in the *Gentleman's Magazine*. Many of the deaths were at an advanced age, fourteen of them over 80 and four over a 100.[15] Smart had prophesied 'that men will live to a much greater age' (C 88), and it seems he may have been looking out for such instances. But to what end?

Many writers go through set procedures, rituals one might call them, before they begin to work, and perhaps this, in the end, is what it had become for Smart: a way of beginning the day and setting things in motion. It is hard to see any other justification. Few of the lines in Fragment D are in any way remarkable, lacking either the beauty or the eccentricity of the earlier sections.

There are no 'For' verses in D and it is possible that there never were, as the responses and the personal details that we have come to expect from them seem to be already included in the 'Let' verses. As usual there are some puns and jokes. The death of Mr Grieve producing the response 'Blessed be the name of the Man of Melancholy' (D 67). And in the next to last line the strange name of Odwell appropriately calls up, 'Blessed be the name of Jesus in singularities and singular mercies' (D 236). This has certainly been a poem of singularities, but a singular mercy was about to be shown to him. Three lines before the end we read, 'God be gracious to John Sherrat' (D 235). Smart wrote that line on 28 January 1763, and it was John Sherratt (*sic*) who rescued him from the madhouse two days later.

On the 27th of that month a committee of the House of Commons had met to look into the conditions in the privately run madhouses. Dr Battie of St Luke's and Mr Munro of Bedlam, who apparently detested Battie,[16] were called as expert witnesses. Statements were made that the House did not like. It must have caused a flutter among the people running such places and it seems that Sherratt seized the opportunity to secure Smart's release. How exactly, we do not know, but in his 'Epistle to John Sherratt, Esq.' it is made to sound like a naval engagement with a good deal of swash-buckle to it.

To run thy keel across the boom,
And save my vessel from her doom,
And cut her from the pirate's port,
Beneath the cannon of the fort,
With colours fresh, and sails unfurl'd,
Was nobly dar'd to beat the world.

(ll. 73–8)

Whatever Sherratt did – and it sounds very unofficial – it worked, and on 30 January, for the first time in over five years, Christopher Smart was completely free.

It could be argued that, if we had the Collected Letters of Christopher Smart, his diaries and his journals, then *Jubilate Agno* would be of far less significance, but letters and diaries are structured and structure is a type of fiction. What we have in *Jubilate Agno* is something quite different. While it is in part, as we have seen, a complex and intricately structured work, the antiphony to that structure, its shadow side as it were, is at times singularly unguarded, with an innocence to it we could not hope to encounter elsewhere. It has moments of brilliance, silliness, drabness, fascination, and beauty, but overall it allows us, perhaps uniquely, to see what happens in a highly independent and creative mind when sumptuousness and aridity and wisdom and unwisdom meet.

3

The Psalms of David

In 1762, or perhaps a little earlier, but almost certainly while he was in Dr Potter's private madhouse in Bethnal Green, Smart wrote:

> By false witnesses convicted
>   That against me were suborn'd,
> I was punish'd and afflicted
>   For the very things I scorn'd.

> (ll. 41–4)

And this is how it must have seemed to him when his wife and father-in-law presented their petition to St Luke's in 1759 and had him committed as insane. It was all wrong. It was a conspiracy. It was false witness. How could they do such a thing to him? He loved his wife, and he had worked hard for his father-in-law on so many of his projects, and not all of them to his liking, yet this was how they treated him in return.

> For good offices, ungrateful,
>   They could evil things return,
> In despite of kindness hateful
>   To my sorrowing soul's concern.

> (ll. 45–8)

It was degrading and humiliating that a onetime Fellow of Pembroke College should have been put away in a madhouse.

> But in my distress they jested,
>   Yea the very abjects met,
> Making mouths, my peace infested
>   Without ceasing or regret.

> Fawning gluttons, in conjunction
> With the mimicking buffoon,
> Gnash their teeth without compunction,
> And my miseries importune.
>
> (ll. 49–56)

We remember those painful lines in *Jubilate Agno*, 'For silly fellow! silly fellow! is against me' (B 60) and 'For they pass by me in their tour' (B 63), and here we read:

> O! let not my foes exulting,
> In defiance of thy laws,
> And with nods and winks insulting,
> Bear me down without a cause.
>
> (ll. 73–6)

We remember too that Mason had thought he was dead, and Gray has predicted that he would end up in 'Jayl or Bedlam' and it as though Smart knew what was being said about him:

> 'All that we surmise has follow'd,'
> Let them not with triumph boast,
> 'His remains the gulph has swallowed,
> He has given up the ghost.'
>
> (ll. 97–100)

But, typically, he forgives all his persecutors, and ends the poem with a renewal of his decision to devote himself to writing poems in praise of God.

> As for me in heavenly phrases
> I will harmonize my tongue,
> Day by day Jehovah's praises
> Shall in sweeter notes be sung.
>
> (ll. 109–12)

If only, at this point, it were possible to give the title of the poem; indeed, if only the poem had a title, because having to identify it as Smart's translation of Psalm 35 changes everything. There is such an entrenched resistance to reading the Bible as one would any other book, and that includes the anthology of 150 lyrics known as the Book of Psalms. However, this subterfuge may at least have suggested that Smart's translations of these psalms do deserve to be read.

37

The interesting thing about this version of Psalm 35 is that, while it appears to be an intensely personal lyric, closely referring to Smart's own situation, it is in fact a very close rendering of the original. Without going back over all the stanzas quoted above and comparing them line by line, three verses will suffice:

11. False witnesses did rise up: they laid to my charge things that I knew not.
15. But in my adversity they rejoiced, and gathered themselves together: yea, the very abjects came together against me unawares, making mouths at me, and ceased not.
19. O let not them that are mine enemies triumph over me ungodly: neither let them wink with their eyes that hate without a cause.[1]

The most concrete elements here – the false witnesses, the very abjects, the making mouths, and the winking – are all present in the original psalm. This is a translation, and yet as we read it and recognize it as being so very close to Smart's own situation, it is hardly possible to believe that he was not aware of it too. This is what gives so many of these poems an added poignancy: that time and again Smart finds the Psalmist sharing his plight and sharing his sufferings. He does not deviate into overpersonal statements or associations, but he does know from first-hand experience what he is writing about.

It would be equally significant, even if less dramatic, were Smart to be found taking pains to avoid the personal element. And such instances exist. As one might expect, any references to madness or being locked up are carefully muted. In Psalm 88 there is a cry of anguish, 'I am in misery, and like unto him that is at the point to die: even from my youth up thy terrors have I suffered with a troubled mind.' Smart deftly sidesteps the offending words:

> Full of pain, with terror shaken,
>   Ev'n as gasping to depart,
> All thy plagues I have partaken
>   Youth and age, with anxious heart.

(ll. 57–60)

These parallels do exist and do entice, but waiting for us almost at the end of the collection are a number of surprises. They begin at Psalm 141, where verse 6 reads, 'But let not their precious balms break my head: yea, I will pray yet against their wickedness.' And Smart not only introduces a non-textual reference to his own psalms, but seemingly to his own name.

> But let not what they give for balm
> Increase my raging smart;
> Nay, I will pray my psalm
> Against their hand and heart.
>
> (ll. 21–4)

In context, of course, *smart* is simply a common noun, but can a writer use a homonym of his own name like this (especially *raging* smart), and not be aware of it? In the next stanza he goes on to compare the sweetness of his verse with the harshness of other prose translations – an idea that bears very little relation to the words of the psalm.

> Let such false judges as commend
> Their harsh precarious prose,
> To this my song attend,
> Which in sweet measure flows.
>
> (ll. 25–8)

7. Let their judges be overthrown in stony places: that they may hear my words, for they are sweet.

Seemingly having decided on a personal statement at this late stage of the work, he does not shy away this time from the mention of confinement in the last verse of Psalm 142.

> Take me from this bondage hateful,
> Which my spirit so dismays,
> That again the good and grateful
> May attend my song of praise.

9. Bring my soul out of prison, that I may give thanks unto thy Name: which thing if thou wilt grant me, then shall the righteous resort unto my company.

The suggestion of a song of praise is there in the Psalter, but is this his own work he is referring to? The concluding verses of the following psalm are also in the same vein.

Lord, from this despondence rousing,
  For the glory of thy name,
And my righteous cause espousing,
  Bring my soul from bonds and shame.

And my foes and evil neighbours,
  Lord, by charity controul;
For I dedicate my labours
  To the Saviour of my soul.

(ll. 41–8)

11. Quicken me, O Lord for thy Name's sake: and for thy
    righteousness' sake bring my soul out of trouble.

12. And of thy goodness slay mine enemies: and destroy all them
    that vex my soul; for I am thy servant.

Smart did dedicate his labours to Christ in the 'Hymn to the
Supreme Being'; his bondage was shameful, and he did
consider his cause to be a righteous one. We do not know if
these closing psalms were written near the time of his release,
but it looks a possibility. Finally on this point, there is another
peculiarity in the second verse of Psalm 142.

Tears and tender strains diffusive,
  I presented as I knelt,
And compos'd my words allusive
  To the troubles which I felt

2. I poured out my complaints before him: and shewed him of my
   trouble.

From Christopher Hunter we learn that 'Mr Smart, in compos-
ing the religious poems, was frequently so impressed with the
sentiment of devotion, as to write particular passages on his
knees'.[2] Is the writer Smart himself? Are the words *allusive* to
the troubles he himself felt?

There is no easy answer, but poets do not choose to translate
other poets unless there is something in the original that
speaks to them. Pope would have us believe it was all by
chance that he came to write his imitations of Horace.
Bolingbroke happened to call, and happened to thumb through
a copy of Horace, which just happened to be lying on the table,
and 'observed how well it would hit my case'.[3] But the urbanity

40

of tone and the cutting wit both poets shared was not a matter of chance.

No one was better placed to speak for David than Smart. Like David, he was a poet; he too was beset by enemies and hardship, and he too loved his god. These translations allow him to speak of these things, and allow him to do so in the first person.

The eighteenth century was a great age of literary translation and imitation. Two of its most accomplished poets, Pope and Cowper, published highly acclaimed translations of Homer, and, while it may be that neither is much read today, that is only to be expected, as each was intended for a contemporary audience and they have been replaced, as generations come and go, by new translations that, whatever their comparative shortcomings, will have had about them the appeal of a new and different contemporaneity.

With imitation it is different. Pope's Horace, like Johnson's imitations of Juvenal, are regarded as poems in their own right and will continue to be read.

To judge from the magazines of the time, imitation of the classics was a popular literary genre, but what we may have lost sight of is that the classical Hebrew poets were once accorded the same serious attention, and were translated by poets as gifted and as various as Sidney, Wyatt, Herbert, Crashaw, Milton, and Pope. They concentrated on *selected* psalms.[4] To undertake the entire Psalter was not only a daunting task; it meant facing up to the problem of those dreadful curses and imprecations that the psalmists brought down on the heads of their enemies; not to mention children's heads being dashed against the stones, and all those people with their teeth broken and their cheekbones smitten. How could all that be reconciled with Christ's command that we love our neighbours?

The violence could always be muffled up in a blend of Augustan gentility, decorum, and euphemism, and this was the method used by Tate and Brady, whose metrical (in truth, doggerel) version of the Psalter had been printed at the back of every Book of Common Prayer since 1696. But their version, despite this official blessing, was never popular and only a few London churches used it. Sad to say, even Brady's own church,

St Catherine Cree, rejected it as 'an innovation not to be endured'.[5]

The Church wanted and needed something better, and, if strict translation had its problems, then the alternatives were imitation, or translation along the lines famously employed by John Dryden, who wrote, 'I have endeavoured to make Virgil speak such English as he would himself have spoken, if he had been born in England, and in this present age'.[6] But, had the Psalmist had the benefit of such advantages, he would not only have been a Christian; in all probability he would have been a member of the Church of England, and so the problem of violence versus the Christian qualities of love and forgiveness is still there. Messianic *interpretation* of the Psalter has a long tradition within the Christian Church, but changing the actual language of the Psalms was quite another matter. They were the word of God.

It was Isaac Watts, in an *Essay towards the Improvement of Christian Psalmody*, in 1707, who claimed to have made the breakthrough. He agreed with the conservatives that the Psalms should be read as God's word to us and ought therefore to be translated as literally as possible, in prose in fact, because rhyme and metre are bound to change the meaning in some way. The important word here though is *read*. When the psalms are read, they are God's word to us; but, when we sing them to God, our chief design is, or should be, to speak our own hearts, therefore using our own words. The argument is simple, but its implications were enormous. If the Psalms were to be made meaningful for all occasions, and Watts cites the obvious difficulty of the Eucharist, then David must be made to speak like a Christian, and an eighteenth-century one at that. Watts claims to be 'the first who hath brought down the royal author into the common affairs of the Christian life, and led the psalmist of Israel into the Church of Christ'.[7]

The argument looks simple. It even looks familiar. Watts is following Dryden. But nothing can have prepared his first readers for the beginning of Psalm 67:

> Shine, mighty God! on Britain shine
> With beams of heav'nly grace ...

Smart's Christianization of the Psalter, though never so extreme, is often extensive and bold. For example, Psalm 54 is a plea for help, in which the Psalmist is beset by strangers and tyrants, and he calls out to God, confident that He will destroy them. The last verse reads, 'For he hath delivered me out of all of my trouble: and mine eye hath seen his desire upon mine enemies.' And it is from such unlikely material that Smart produced a poem on the agony of Christ in the garden of Gethsemane. What is astonishing is that he has done so without taking any extreme liberties with the text. Each stanza picks up some hint from its counterpart in the Psalter and then develops it. The Psalter begins:

1. Save me, O God, for thy Name's sake: and avenge me in thy strength.
2. Hear my prayer, O God: and hearken unto the words of my mouth.

The imaginative leap Smart makes is to turn David into Christ and so the words of his mouth are the words spoken by Christ in the garden as they are recorded in Matthew 26: 39.

> O God, the name to which I pray,
>   Of boundless love and pow'r,
> O pass, if possible, away,
>   This bitter cup and hour.
>
> Yet if these drops must thus be spilt,
>   Thou, Father, knowest best:
> And be it rather as thou wilt,
>   Than to my soul's request.
>
> (ll. 1–8)

In stanza 3 the strangers and the tyrants of the Psalter have become Herod and Pilate, and with brilliant economy the assault becomes the Crucifixion itself.

> Lo! strangers to thy truth arise,
>   Nor put their trust in thee;
> And Herod, leagu'd with Pilate, vies
>   To nail me to the tree.
>
> (ll. 9–12)

In the next stanza the words 'uphold my soul' are enough in Smart's view to symbolize the Resurrection.

> But God shall raise from stripes and scorn
>   The Lamb betray'd and kill'd;
> And on the third triumphant morn
>   This temple shall rebuild.

(ll. 13–16)

This allows the destruction of the Psalmist's enemies in verse 5 of the Psalter to be changed into love, and so we have the Redemption.

> Then thou shalt greater grace supply
>   To have the worst redeem'd;
> And truth shall make them free to die
>   For him they once blasphem'd.

(ll. 17–20)

The suggestion of a sacrifice in verse 6, 'An offering of a free heart', is given a new significance, and the speaking voice now seems to belong to both Christ and Smart equally.

> A victim patient and resign'd
>   I for the cross prepare,
> And bless thy name, because I find
>   Such consolation there.

(ll. 21–4)

By the time we reach the violence of the final verse of the Psalter, 'mine eye hath seen his desire upon mine enemies', it seems inevitable that it should be translated into the forgiveness of sins.

> For he hath caus'd me to respire,
>   And all my vows have thriv'n;
> Mine eye hath seen my heart's desire
>   In every foe forgiv'n.

(ll. 25–8)

The ground of the original psalm may still be detected, but with the most delicate, sensitive, and intelligent brushwork Smart has painted over all the unpleasant features of the Old Testament and left us with a picture of the central events of

Christianity. This is what he meant in his subtitle to the collection when he said that they were psalms 'Attempted in the Spirit of Christianity'. As with Pope's versions of Horace, the resultant work can be read as a new poem, but with enriched significance because of its dual nature.

Similar methods are employed by Smart to record, or to call attention to, most of the major events in the life of Christ, the starting point often being what would seem at first to be a singularly unpropitious verse. The most audacious variation of all occurs in Psalm 7: 15. Smart has been following the original quite closely until he comes upon a passage dealing with sin, and, where the psalm reads, 'Behold, he travaileth with mischief: he hath conceived sorrow, and brought forth ungodliness', the connotations of these three verbs are transformed into an announcement of the Virgin Birth. In context the effect is startling. Smart's version of the passage becomes:

> Behold a virgin has conceiv'd,
> By congress undefil'd,
> And lost Jeshurun is retriev'd
> By an almighty child.

(ll. 57–60)

Psalm 72 provides him with a much more obvious opportunity. It is written in honour of a king who, it appears, has just acceded to the throne, and it expresses the wishes of his people for a prosperous and peaceful reign. The transition to the King of Heaven is a straightforward one. Watts's version is 'Jesus shall reign where'r the sun'. But Smart makes a nativity hymn out of it, taking advantage of the mention of kings and presents in verse 10 to introduce the frankincense and myrrh.

> They of Tharsis gifts shall offer,
> Sheba's kings, and isles remote,
> Sages from th' Arabian coffer,
> Myrrh and frankincense devote.

(ll. 37–40)

The Resurrection is featured again in Psalm 16: 11. Christ's victory over sin and the Devil is the theme of Psalm 85, and the Ascension is celebrated in 47: 5, where the Psalmist's words

45

'God is gone up with a merry noise: and the Lord with the sound of the trump' become:

> Christ is gone up, the king of kings,
> And joyful acclamation rings,
>   As thankless earth he spurns;
> The marshall'd cherubs stand in rows,
> From inmost heav'n the trumpet blows
>   While God from death returns.

(ll. 25–30)

It is not only the historical events of Christianity that Smart incorporates into his new version; the tenets of the faith are there too, and very often expressed in the actual words that Christ used in his teaching. In his introduction Smart wrote that, 'as it was written with an especial view to the divine service, the reader will find sundry allusions to the rites and ceremonies of the Church of England, which are intended to render the work in general more useful and acceptable to congregations'. Accordingly there are versions that refer to the sacraments of Baptism (87: 7) and of Confirmation (119: Lamed stanza 6).

> From baptism my god-childhood vow,
> From confirmation until now
>   I am enlisted thine;
> Save me, who with the price am bought,
> For I with diligence have sought
>   The way thy laws injoin.

(ll. 31–6)

And on at least half a dozen occasions he provides something to meet one of the Church's greatest needs by adapting verses to make them suitable for the Eucharist.

> Mine infirmities uncloaking
>   I will my confession make,
> At thy shrine thy grace invoking,
>   As thine eucharist I take.

(116: 45–8)

What most distinguishes Smart, however, and gives his version of the Psalms its distinctive flavour is his treatment of the brutality and violence of the Old Testament. Watts either omits it altogether, or else deflects it, blunting it and taking the sting out of it, but Smart's method is more daring. In his introduction he had written, 'In this translation, all expressions, that seem contrary to Christ, are omitted, and evangelical matter put in their room.' One might say that he accepted without reservation the injunction in Matthew 5: 44: 'Love your enemies, bless them that curse you, do good to them that hate you, and pray for them which despitefully use you, and persecute you.' In his psalms all the curses, the hatred, and the brutality are replaced by love, and by prayers of intercession for his enemies.

The vengeful warrior-god of the Old Testament is erased completely and in his place stands the loving and forgiving father of the New. Where the Psalter demands, 'Let them be confounded and perish that are against my soul; let them be covered with shame and dishonour that seek to do me evil,' Smart prays:

> Yet for all their deeds despiteful,
> Keep them from eternal shame;
> And disgrace and pain so rightful
> Let them 'scape in Christ his name.

> (71: 41–4)

By hundreds of deft touches such as these Smart manages to transform the whole tone of the Psalter. The soldier's shield becomes a 'weapon of the spirit / Faith's invulnerable shield' (35: 5–6), the 'two-edged sword' is changed into 'triumphant palms' (149: 36). Psalm 137, which begins so lyrically, 'By the waters of Babylon we sat down and wept,' no longer ends with children being thrown against the stones. Instead we have:

> But he is greatest and the best,
> Who spares his enemies profest,
>   And Christian mildness owns;
> Who gives his captives back their lives,
> Their hapless infants, weeping wives,
>   And for his sins atones.

> (ll. 49–54)

But perhaps the finest of these changes comes in Psalm 7, where the Hebrew god whets his sword and bends his bow.

47

Smart turns the weapon into a rainbow and reminds us instead of God's covenant with Noah.

> Yet e'en to those that love the dark,
>   His vengeance will be slow;
> For pity built the floating ark,
>   And goodness bent his bow.

(ll. 49–52)

To some extent, translating the whole of the Book of Psalms could be said to be tantamount to offering to rewrite *Hamlet*. There are certain psalms and passages from psalms that are so well known and where the prose versions in the Book of Common Prayer and in the Bible are rightly famous and recognized as being an outstanding literary achievement. However, if we look at where the competition is at its most severe – Psalm 23 – Smart can at least stand the comparison.

> Thou shalt my plenteous board appoint
>   Before the braving foe;
> Thine oil and wine mine head anoint
>   And make my goblet flow.

(ll. 17–20)

There is a simplicity and directness here that are much to his credit, and his metrical facility is evident from the fact that he offers an alternative version and deftly changes from the Common Metre quatrain into the romance six of the *Song to David* stanza.

> Thou shalt add plenty to thy grace,
> And heap my board before their face,
>   My troublers to confound;
> The head that thou hast lifted up,
> Thou hast anointed, and the cup
>   Of my salvation crown'd.

(ll. 25–30)

Many of these psalms seem to demand to be sung, and, although it was not to be, Smart himself had performance very much in mind. He knew how glad a congregation is to have variety in its services and there are in fact no less than twenty-five different verse forms in his collection, and at the end of it he does not forget to provide twenty-five different versions of the Gloria, a quite astonishing technical achievement in itself.

In *Jubilate Agno* Smart had written, 'I pray for a musician or musicians to set the new psalms' (D 217), and this prayer, which he had made in 1763, was to receive a generous answer two years later when J. Walsh, a bookseller who specialized in the publication of music, brought out *A Collection of Melodies for the Psalms of David According to the Version of Christopher Smart, M.A. by the most eminent Composers of Church Music.* There were forty-five melodies, and the composers were indeed eminent men. They included William Boyce, Master of His Majesty's Band of Musick, Benjamin Cooke, the Organist of Westminster Abbey, James Nares, Master of the Children of His Majesty's Chapel Royal, John Randall, Professor of Music and organist of King's College Cambridge, and many more. It can hardly have looked more promising, but the collection was never reprinted and there is no evidence that it was ever used widely or gained even the slightest popularity.

Smart had also written in *Jubilate Agno*, 'I pray God to bless all my subscribers' (D 221), and at the time of publication there were 736 of them to be blessed. To read through their names is to follow the story of his life, and it is remarkable the number of distinguished people who, in spite of all his 'difficulties', still regarded him highly enough to wish to be included in the list: writers, scholars, painters, musicians, generals, lords, bishops, and even the Chief Justice of Florida. The aristocratic patrons of his early days are there: half a dozen members of the Vane family, the Delavals, the Earl of Darlington, and the Duke of Cleveland. Also we find the friends he made during his time at Cambridge: his tutor, Leonard Addison, Roger Long, the Master of Pembroke, and even, rather surprisingly, Thomas Gray. Old feuds, it seems, had been forgotten. And of course John Sherratt's name is there. There is a host of writers and artists he knew in London. Among them we find Akenside, Churchill, Charles Burney, Hogarth, Garrick, the Whartons, Smollett, and Lowth. And then there is William Cowper, one of the most interesting names on the list, for Cowper himself had been in Dr Cotton's asylum in St Albans until June of that year. There is evidence that Smart and Cowper knew each other,[8] and this is a pleasing link between two of the finest poets of the century.

The names that are not on the list have their interest too. Smart's mother, his sisters, and his brother-in-law all subscribed, but not his wife. Also missing are the names of Newbery and Carnan, who were publishing a rival translation by James Merrick.

It had all looked promising. Smart had done everything that could be expected of him, but the Church took no notice of his book, and, far from being the success he had hoped for, the volume even contributed to his final downfall. Not long after its publication, his printer, the wealthy and influential Dryden Leach, had him arrested for a debt of £86.[9] Presumably Smart had spent the subscription money. Someone paid the debt for him, but signs of the troubles ahead are there.

The contemporary critical response was equally disastrous. Smart had unwisely attacked the *Monthly Review* for its adverse criticism of his *Poems* of 1763, and their response was particularly cutting: 'some unhappy circumstances in this gentleman's life, seem to have given his latter writings a peculiar claim to total exemption from criticism. Accordingly we chuse to be silent with regard to the merits of the present publication.'[10] It was an eloquent and damning silence with just enough innuendo in those words 'unhappy circumstances'. The *Critical Review* compared Smart's version with James Merrick's, recommending Merrick and lumping Smart in with 'a crowd of wretched poets, who have overwhelmed [the Psalmist's] native grace and dignity under the rubbish of their despicable schemes'.[11]

Smart had generously prayed for Merrick in *Jubilate Agno* (D 203) and it was Merrick's version that went into a second edition and whose verses were chosen by Gregory to go into his translation of Lowth's *Lectures on Hebrew Poetry*, despite the fact that his favoured octosyllabic couplets could be as bad as

> Ill for my Good return'd I find,
> Nor know from ought (but that, inclin'd
> To Good, their deeds I shun,) to date
> The grounds of their preposterous hate.[12]

Smart's version was not even thought highly of by his own relations. Christopher Hunter could only see fit to include one psalm in his collection of 1791, the Second Version of Psalm 148, and even then he made alterations of his own. All the rest he dismissed as bearing 'for the most part melancholy proofs of the recent estrangement of his mind'.[13] Elizabeth Le Noir, Smart's younger daughter, published a collection of her own poems in 1826 and at the end of the second volume she included some of her father's hymns (again 'improved'), but she prefaced them by saying

> The following HYMNS were written by CHRISTOPHER SMART, and are selected from a collection at the end of his Version of the Psalms, published in 1765, and honoured by a most numerous and respectable subscription: they are, very little known; for these Psalms are far from being among the best of his works; and it is probable that few readers would labour through their thick shade to the flowers that precede and conceal. The Authoress, though his Daughter, had not been induced to do so.[14]

The term 'serpent's tooth' comes to mind. She is right, of course, when she says that *The Psalms* are far from being the best of his works, but had she been induced to read them she might have agreed that there are flowers among them that deserve rather more than to blush unseen. They were the quarry from which he worked *A Song to David*, but she dismissed that too.

4

A Song to David

Within three weeks of his release from Dr Potter's madhouse, Smart had already begun a publicity campaign for the work he had written during all those years of confinement and silence. Proposals for a subscription edition of his translation of *The Psalms* had appeared in the *Daily Advertiser* as early as 21 February 1763 and it was probably only the difficulties involved in gathering together so many subscribers – there were eventually 736 of them – that delayed its publication until 1765. *A Song to David*, a quarto of two dozen pages, presented less of a problem and no time was lost. Notice of its publication first appeared in the *Public Advertiser* on 6 April 1763, when he had been free for only nine weeks.

The initial reaction of the leading literary journals was not hostile. It was worse. It was patronizing and dismissive. The *Monthly Review* began by hailing it as 'irregularly great'[1] but then delivered the death blow by launching the story of the wainscot and the key, while the *Critical Review* branded it as 'a fine piece of ruins'.[2] Had Smart been able to stay calm and let the poem speak for him, he might have been able to re-establish something of his reputation among his readers, but calm was not a quality he had ever been renowned for. He was incensed, and naming names he rounded on his critics, vociferously, and in print.[3] The result was only to be expected. Fighting back, both journals ignored the poem and went for the man.

The *Monthly* quoted some lines from *Samson Agonistes*:

> By how much from the top of wondrous glory,
> To lowest pitch of abject fortune thou art fallen.

and promised, seeing they had upset him so, to ignore him totally in future.[4] But, if the *Monthly* had done with him, the *Critical Review* had not: 'Our sentiments with regards to this unfortunate gentleman are such as every man must feel on the same melancholy occasion. If our readers are desirous to know what they are, we must refer them to the fine lines at the end of Mr Churchill's epistle to Hogarth.'[5]

On the surface this sounds kindly enough, but when we turn to the lines themselves, which had been published only a short time before, the truth is very different.

> And sunk, deep sunk, in second childhood's night!
> Are men indeed such things? and are the best
> More subject to this evil than the rest,
> To drivel out whole years of idiot breath,
> And sit the monuments of living death?

It was a cruel attack and with hindsight we can see how successful it was. Smart was as good as finished. Almost everything he wrote after 1763 bore the stigma of insanity. *A Song to David* almost disappeared from sight. The compilers of two major anthologies, Robert Anderson (1795) and Alexander Chalmers (1810), could find no more than the stanzas the *Monthly* had printed in its review. In 1826, when Smart's younger daughter, Elizabeth Le Noir, published her own *Miscellaneous Poems*, she included some of her father's poems, but not the *Song*. She was icily scathing about that. 'The poem contains some fine lines; but all a daughter's partiality could not lead the writer of this to admire it, nor all her pains, after many perusals, discover the beauties with which, when supposed lost, it was so liberally endowed.'[6] She even unkindly suggested that it owed its celebrity to the fact that people did think it was lost.

Then everything changed. After 1887, when Browning took up the cause in his *Parleyings with Certain People of Importance in their Day*, this poem, which had been ridiculed and dismissed, was turned around full circle and came to be regarded not only as a masterpiece but as the only poem by Smart that was worth looking at. By the end of the century, it was being argued that, 'This poem stands alone, the most extraordinary phenomenon, perhaps, in our literature, the one rapt strain in the poetry of the eighteenth century, the work of a poet who, though he produced much, has not produced elsewhere a single line which indicates the power here displayed.'[7] But – and this in no way lessens the magnitude of its achievement – *A Song to David* is not unique, either in terms of Smart's poetry as a whole, or in terms of the poetry of his time.

When the *Song* dominated whatever critical attention was given to Smart there was a tendency to regard the romance six as being peculiarly its own verse form. But it was the form of the regular ode and was used as such by Akenside, Shenstone, Cowper, Collins, and many others besides Smart. Within his own work this stanza was certainly not peculiar to the *Song*. Thirty of his psalms, the first and the last, and also Psalm 119, which is itself divided into twenty-two separate parts, are written in this form. The very real danger of associating the stanza too closely with Smart was seen when Robert Brittain, his first truly scholarly editor, was deceived into attributing to him an unsigned 'Benedicite Paraphrased'.[8] On the face of it, it did seem a convincing attribution, but turned out to have been written by, of all people, James Merrick, Smart's rival translator of the Psalms.

Smart's preoccupation with David has been described as 'manic',[9] but in the eighteenth century it would not have been thought of as so very unusual. For most of us David is probably no more than a dim, possibly legendary figure from some remote biblical past. We remember that he killed Goliath with a slingshot, that he soothed Saul's rages by playing the harp to him, that there was something dubious about his relationship with Bathsheba, and that he may, or may not, have composed the Psalms. For the eighteenth century it was different and not simply because they knew their Bibles better than we do. David was at that time very much a live issue, a figure of controversy, with several books and pamphlets written about him.

The controversy may be seen as having begun in 1710 with Pierre Bayle's *An Historical and Critical Dictionary*, a book that Smart is known to have borrowed from his college library. In it Bayle grants that David was 'one of the greatest Men in the world', but not where virtue was concerned. His murder of

Uriah and subsequent adultery with Bathsheba made it quite impossible for him to be regarded as a man 'after God's own Heart'.[10] Such an attack on a biblical figure was certain to cause a furore, and Patrick Delany, on the title page of his three-volume *Life of David*, promised to reply to Bayle's criticisms. And he did, calling him 'a known patron of all errors that ever obtained in the world from its foundation'.[11] Delany, whose book Smart had also taken from the library, acknowledged David's sins – they were a matter of fact – but stressed the great example his repentance provided us with. 'Millions have fallen, have sinned, as David did, but who ever repented and recovered like him? Revolve his whole life before this evil accident, it is almost one train of a wise, a generous, a pious, and a valiant conduct!'[12] We can see which side Smart is on: stanza XVI of the *Song* begins 'Wise – in recovery from his fall'.

It may be appropriate to add at this point that Delany's importance to Smart does not lie solely in his attitude to David's life. He can also be seen as having influenced the very centre of Smart's thinking and writing, as, when dealing with David's song of thanksgiving in I Chronicles 16, he says:

> after *David* hath exhorted the people to praise and to give thanks to GOD, for his peculiar mercies to them there recited, he then breaks out into a rapture of gratitude, in contemplation of the infinite bounty and benignity of the Creator, and calls upon the whole of Creation, to fill up the chorus of his praise.[13]

There could hardly be a more succinct summation of Smart's own approach not only to poetry but to God.

Smart was in Dr Potter's madhouse when the controversy moved into its next phase, but, as we have seen, he was not unaware of what was going on outside. It began with a sermon preached by the Revd Samuel Chandler on the death of George II. Taking up the epitaph on David at the end of the First Book of Chronicles, it was entitled *The Character of a great and good King full of Days, Riches, and Honour.* Comparing the lives and deaths of the two monarchs, he showers them both with every conceivable virtue and in such fulsome tones that a waggish reply was inevitable, and it came in the form of an anonymous pamphlet, *The Life of David, or the History of the Man after God's own Heart*, which elaborated on all David's various sins instead and proclaimed, 'This, Britons! is the king to whom your late excellent Monarch has been compared! What an impiety to the Majesty of Heaven! What an affront to the memory of an honest Prince!' The pamphlet was refuted and the refutation challenged, with Chandler expanding his sermon into a work of two whole volumes published posthumously in 1766. As Professor Sherbo says, after detailing all these comings and goings and huffings and puffings, 'there was a timeliness about the appearance of the *Song* that should have insured it a greater degree of success and attention than it gained'.[14]

Smart, not surprisingly, is on the side of the angels in this debate. The poem begins quietly. Its first three stanzas are an invocation in which David is presented to us enthroned in heaven, playing on his harp and singing hymns of praise and gratitude. The opening of the *Song* therefore lays the groundwork for two of its major themes: that of David being the supreme poet of all time and that true praise is the expression of gratitude. The invocation ends with an invitation to David, the praise-singer and author of the great book of Gratitude, to receive, in his turn, the praise that Smart is about to bestow on him.

Bayle, Chandler, and the others had argued at length over David's sins, the murder and the adultery, but for Smart it is as though such events had never taken place. They scarcely receive a mention. In stanza IV it is his virtues, or, in the words of the Contents, 'the excellence and lustre of David's character', that he lists. It is a list that features the same twelve virtues (with one slight change of *Serene* for *Happy*) he had included, and in the same order, in *Jubilate Agno* (B 601–13), where each virtue was attributed to one of the sons of Jacob. For example, Reuben is Great, Simeon is Valiant, and so on. David is therefore presented to us in this stanza as the embodiment of all that was finest among the twelve tribes of Israel. He is, we are told:

> Great, valiant, pious, good, and clean,
> Sublime, contemplative, serene,
>   Strong, constant, pleasant, wise!
> Bright effluence of exceeding grace;
> Best man! – the swiftness and the race,
>   The peril, and the prize!

(ll. 19–24)

Each of the following twelve stanzas then elaborates on one of these virtues, combining with dexterity and economy of expression threads from a variety of different sources. To begin with, David's greatness lies most clearly in that he was a king, and stanza V brings together accounts from both Chronicles and the Book of Samuel, telling of his acclamation by the elders and the people of Israel after the death of Saul, as well as his anointing by Samuel when he was still a child; while at the same time incorporating two phrases from Smart's own translation of the Psalms: 'from rear to van' (53: 47) and 'the man of God's own choice' (21: 3), which, considered in their original context, bring with them their own apposite connotations. As well as the Bible, Chapter 10 of Delany's *Life of David*, entitled 'David designs to build a Temple', is a direct source for the ideas and also for much of the language in stanza VII on David's piety.[15] Mention of the Temple introduces another thread: that of Smart's Freemasonry. In *Jubilate Agno* he had asserted

For I am the Lord's builder and free and accepted MASON in CHRIST JESUS.

(B 109)

In his *Lexicon of Freemasonry* A. G. Mackey devotes several pages to a consideration of Solomon's Temple, explaining that, although Solomon built it, it was David who planned it, and David was not only therefore to be regarded as a Mason, but as possibly having been the first Grand Master.

We also read in Mackey that 'There are in Freemasonry twelve original points which form the basis of the system, and comprehend the whole ceremony of initiation. These twelve points refer the twelve parts of the ceremony of initiation to the twelve tribes of Israel.'[16] The appearance of both these concepts within the opening lines of Smart's *A Song to David* cannot be without significance, and it is a thread that will be taken up later.

Within stanzas V–XVI there are references to most of the important events in David's life. We see him as a boy tending his father's flocks and defending them against the lion and the bear. He slays Goliath and is anointed by Samuel. He spares the life of Saul in the cave at En-gedi, when he could so easily have killed him. We are reminded of his love for Jonathan and how he forgave Shimei, who cursed him and threw stones at him. And there is even a passing reference – though not by name – to Bathsheba. It was an eventful life. David was a man of immense vitality with so many sides to his character. And this must have been one of the attractions he had for Smart. For, just as Smart saw the multiplicity of the created universe, bird, beast and fish, plant and gem, from the most common-place to the most exotic, coming together to praise God, so David can be seen to represent, through the diversity of his character, the totality of the perfect man.

It is in stanza IX where this is most apparent.

> Clean – if perpetual prayer be pure,
> And love, which could itself innure
>   To fasting and to fear –
> Clean in his gestures, hands, and feet,
> To smite the lyre, the dance compleat,
>   To play the sword and spear.
>
> (ll. 49–54)

Clean was evidently a word with some complexity of meaning for Smart. In *Jubilate Agno*, where the virtues are linked with the sons of Jacob, *Clean* is the only one to be given some further definition. 'For Dan is Clean – neat, dextrous, apt, active, compact' (B 606). They are unexpectedly wide-ranging associations, with *active* being the most unexpected, but in this stanza David is at his most active. He is a man of prayer, a lover, a musician, a dancer, and a warrior, and the stanza ends with the unusual transposition of verbs, which seems to emphasize the homogeneity of his actions and his skills: it is the lyre that he *smites*, while the sword is what he *plays*.

David's life was not one of physical activity alone; Smart shows in these stanzas that he was equally renowned for his moral and intellectual excellence. He had the inner strength to 'defy Satan' (l. 74). He was constant in his love of God (l. 79) and had the wisdom to repent when he had done wrong (l. 91). But he was also the 'best poet which ever lived', and in this he was:

> Sublime – invention ever young,
> Of vast conception, tow'ring tongue,
>   To God th' eternal theme;

Notes from yon exaltations caught,
Unrival'd royalty of thought,
O'er meaner strains supreme.

(ll. 55–60)

Sublime is a word that has slithered out of precise use in our own vocabulary, but in Lowth's *Lectures* it was of sufficient importance to merit several chapters. He wrote:

> Sublimity of sentiment may be accounted a distinct quality, and may be said to proceed, either from a certain elevation of the mind, and a happy boldness of conception, or from a strong impulse of the soul, when agitated by the most violent affections . . . That species of the sublime which proceeds from a boldness of spirit and an elevation of the soul . . . is displayed, first, in the greatness and sublimity of the subject itself; secondly, in the choice of the adjuncts or circumstances . . . and lastly, in the splendour and magnificence of the imagery by which the whole is illustrated.[17]

Although he goes on to say that it is only truly to be found among the Hebrew writers, we might argue with him now and suggest that it is a term that could be applied not only to David but also to *A Song to David*.

From the perfections of David's life, Smart moves on to the perfections of his poetry, and once again he uses the rhetorical device of statement and amplification, which allows him to work in the way in which he wrote best, in small units, stanza by stanza. David's themes are – and one stanza is devoted to each – God, the angels, man, and the world, followed by planets, birds, fishes, beasts, and gems. It is very reminiscent of *Jubilate Agno* and indeed Smart and David are seen to be very alike in their approach, employing the words of man to praise the universe, which was itself created by the word of God.

Dualities and opposites are everywhere in this section. There is the active 'ministry' of the guardian angels, while others sit and play on their 'citterns', or harps. Man – made in the 'semblance' of God – 'rules' over the land and the sea, but is also 'laborious' in His praise. The world itself has both 'glorious light' and 'soothing shade'. There are plants for our use and plants for our delight: those of 'virtuous root' and the 'sweetners of the gale'. Then there are the birds.

> Of fowl – e'en ev'ry beak and wing
> Which chear the winter, hail the spring,
>   That live in peace or prey;
> They that make music, or that mock,
> The quail, the brave domestic cock,
>   The raven, swan, and jay.

(ll. 133–8)

There are some that are with us all through the winter, while others return with the spring. There are birds of prey and birds of peace. Some make sweet music; others 'mock'. Some are brave like the cock, and some, like the tiny quail, are less so. And in the last line, of the raven and the swan – both 'unclean' according to Deuteronomy (14: 14, 16) – one is black, and one is white, while the jay is an exotic mix of so many colours. It is a stanza Hopkins would surely have liked.

The stanza on the beasts has a different kind of variety: work and play.

> Of beasts – the beaver plods his task;
> While the sleek tygers roll and bask,
>   Nor yet the shades arouse:
> Her cave the mining coney scoops;
> Where o'er the mead the mountain stoops,
>   The kids exult and brouse.

(ll. 145–50)

The beaver is plodding away busily among its heavy consonants, while in a line of liquids and long sensuous vowels 'the sleek tygers roll and bask'. The second half of the stanza takes up Psalm 104: 18: 'The high hills are a refuge for the wild goats: and so are the stony rocks for the conies.' Smart has introduced a further contrast here between the mountain and the mead. The coney is digging out her burrow, while the kids are happily eating and frisking about on the hilltops. There is nothing judgemental about this, nor was there in the stanza about the birds. Work and play are both to be enjoyed; the different creatures praise God according to their different natures.

Even inanimate nature is capable of equal diversity: shining down in the dark of the earth are the gems. Some have use and others value and among them is the topaz, whose veins, as we were told in 'Immensity', seem to portray 'a living landskip' and so bear 'the master's stamp'.

Each century has seemed to declare its own predilections by its attitude to the *Song* and the twentieth century's preference for ambiguity and difficulty has been shown in its concentration on the stanzas that Smart described in his Contents as showing that 'the pillars of knowledge are the monuments of God's work in the first week'. An Appendix in the Oxford Edition of Smart's *Poetical Works* begins, 'Without doubt the most complex, the most obscure and the most discussed passage in *A Song to David* is that on the seven pillars' (*PW* ii. 148). In truth the stanzas themselves are neither complex nor obscure; the only obscurity is the seven Greek letters with which they begin, and it is these letters – not even the stanzas they introduce – which have been the centre of so much discussion.

These seven letters – alpha, gamma, eta, theta, iota, sigma, and omega – do not spell out a word and are not an anagram of a word. Christopher Devlin favoured numerology, arguing that 'the letters should be taken as the numbers for which they stand in classical Greek'.[18] Alpha is number one and provides us with no difficulty. Gamma, being three, denotes spiritual perfection. We can accept this because of the Trinity. Eta is seven, which he says is three upon four and signifies perfect growth, three for perfection of soul, four for bodily perfection, and seven is the union of both. This looks problematic, but sigma is eighteen and, while he admits that it appears to have no significance whatsoever, this did not persuade him to abandon his system.

Another writer, Francis D. Adams, stayed with the numbers theory but suggested that they refer to the corresponding psalms in Smart's own translation.[19] One of the characteristics of such ingenious theories is that, when they fail to work, it is the poet who gets the blame. Adams says, 'In the fourth stanza Smart lost control of these complexities . . . the link is not as satisfactory as the earlier ones'.[20] He does not seem to see that it is his theory that is wrong, not the poem.

By far the most erudite contribution to the debate is that of K. M. Rogers,[21] who has drawn parallels with Cabalistic works that show that most of the letters of the Hebrew alphabet represent a name of God, and she suggests that these Hebrew letters were transliterated by Smart into Greek. It is an argument too complex to summarize, but at the end of it I find myself in agreement with the critic who said it made her 'wonder, especially when one is offered Egyptian as well as Hebrew, Greek and English characters, whether Katherine Rogers is not displaying her own great learning rather than Smart's'.[22]

Rogers also suggested parallels with Masonic imagery, and this needs to be given some consideration, as the fundamental symbolism of these stanzas is architectural. They are 'the pillars of the Lord', and He 'drew the plan', and 'accomplished the design'. It is the *shape* of the Greek letters that is related to the Masonic symbols. Alpha can be seen as a pair of compasses, one of the three main pieces of 'furniture' in a Masonic Lodge. Gamma is shaped like a set square, which is another of the 'immovable jewels' set in the east of a Lodge. Rogers writes that eta and theta do not figure in Masonry, but eta can represent the rung of a ladder and Jacob's theological ladder, each rung of which is a special virtue, is a common Masonic symbol. And theta is the point within the circle, which Mackey explains is a symbol of the sun and is in every 'well regulated Lodge'. Iota looks like a plumb line, but appears to have no particular link with the stanza it introduces, and finding a place for sigma in the Masonic or Cabalistic scheme of things is where Rogers is at her most abstruse.

What is clear, as one considers these symbols, is that in choosing them Smart overturned a cornucopia of both orthodox and esoteric religious thought and that there seems no end to the possibilities. For example, remembering that sigma is eighteen, a look into Cruden's Concordance reveals that, when Solomon built a house for Pharaoh's daughter (1 Kgs. 7: 8–15), he engaged Hiram of Tyre, who was 'a widow's son' (an important Masonic term) and who was 'filled with wisdom', and Hiram cast 'two pillars of brass, of eighteen cubits high apiece'. The evidence is there, and, as far as I am aware, it is my very own discovery; nevertheless I do not believe a word of it. It would appear that we find whatever we go looking for and there is a line in *Jubilate Agno* warning us that 'the mind of man cannot bear a tedious accumulation of nothings without effect' (C 35).

When *A Song to David* first appeared and was reviewed in the *Monthly*, these were the stanzas that came in for scrutiny and exegesis even then, and John Langhorne offered this explanation.

> Few Readers probably will see into the Author's reason for distinguishing his seven pillars or monuments of the six days creation, by the seven Greek letters he hath selected. These, we conjecture, are made choice of, as consecrated for the following reasons. *Alpha* and *Omega* from a well-known text in the Revelation. *Iota, Eta* and *Sigma*, because they are used to signify our Saviour, on altars and pulpits. *Theta*, as being the initial of *Theos*, (in Greek) God; and *Gamma*, as denoting the number *three*, held sacred by some Christians.[23]

Admittedly the letters found on altars are not in the order Smart puts them in, but Smart's whole sequence is in alphabetical order with alternate vowels and consonants and that is a sufficient kind of order in itself. That Smart did not challenge this reading may be significant too in view of his angry reaction to other aspects of the review. Langhorne's interpretation has several points in its favour: it is contemporary and it is what any reader of average intelligence would be expected to recognize. It is also simple and it makes sense in relation to the section as a whole, and therefore, if only for our peace of mind, it might be wisest to accept it.

With so many architectural references, this is a moment in the poem that is certainly monumental, but it has to be admitted that the events of creation are presented here in a language that is disappointingly uneventful, and heavily reliant on stock diction such as 'fleet clouds' and 'saffron robe'. On the pillar for the third day there are 'verdant carvings'. 'Th' illustrious lights' are there on the fourth and the birds and the fish that Smart described elsewhere in such detail become simply 'those that fly' and 'he that swims', while animal life is reduced to 'the social droves'. What these stanzas do not do is bring creation to life for us, but, with the rest of the *Song* being so abundant in vitality, it might be that Smart was aiming for something different here.

God created everything in the universe. That was His plan. He created – and Smart's stanzas naturally follow this order –

light, heaven and earth, the planets and the stars, the birds, the fish, the beasts and man. And He created man in His own image.

> Fair on whose face, and stately frame,
> Did God impress his hallow'd name,
>   For ocular belief.

(ll. 214–16)

But in addition to this plan, He also had a design.

> His wisdom drew the plan;
> His WORD accomplish'd the design,
> From brightest gem to deepest mine,
> From CHRIST enthron'd to man.

(ll. 177–80)

Their capital letters bring WORD and CHRIST together. This is the Word made Flesh. It is the design of the Incarnation. God drew the plan of creation, but the realization of His design would eventually be accomplished in man through Christ. He would be encouraged, inspired, to follow Christ, and to make the 'bold attempt and brave advance' which that involves. And the Sabbath Day the 'GREATEST and the BEST' was, Smart explains, given to man to have time to rest and to think about this and to express his gratitude.

These seven stanzas can therefore be seen to contain some of Smart's most deeply held beliefs and themes: the creation by God of a universe of awesome diversity; the inseparability of the God of the Old Testament and the God of the New; and the obligation upon man to express not only his own gratitude but to voice that of the universe as a whole. It is familiar ground approached from an unfamiliar angle. It is not the uniqueness of this section, nor of the *Song* itself, that needs to be emphasized, but the way in which it epitomizes Smart's thinking over almost two decades.

The next section, described in the Contents as 'an exercise upon the decalogue', is a further example of the Old Testament being viewed and interpreted in the light of the New, as the Commandments of the Mosaic Law have all their negatives replaced by the positives of the Sermon on the Mount, with the result that this moral law becomes not only more benevolent but more hopeful.

Thou art – to give and to confirm,
For each his talent and his term;
  All flesh thy bounties share:
Thou shalt not call thy brother fool;
The porches of the Christian school
  Are meekness, peace, and pray'r.

(241–6)

The Old Testament commandment is expanded so as to include not only God but man, incorporating two of the most important of the Beatitudes, 'Blessed are the meek', and 'Blessed are the peacemakers', together with Christ's warning that 'whoever shall say, Thou fool, shall be in danger of hell fire' (Matt. 5: 22), the latter having a particular poignancy in view of *Jubilate Agno* (B 60), 'For silly fellow! silly fellow! is against me . . .'.

The Fifth Commandment, 'Honour thy father and mother', might be expected to have been sufficiently benign for Smart to have accepted into his own system without change, but he adapts it to include Christ's acceptance of his Father's will in the Garden of Gethsemane.

Rise up before the hoary head,
And God's benign commandment dread,
  Which says thou shalt not die:
'Not as I will, but as thou wilt,'
Pray'd He whose conscience knew no guilt;
  With whose bless'd pattern vie.

(ll. 253–8)

We are to honour the Father, but also the Son, who promised us that, 'He that believeth in me hath everlasting life' (John 6: 47).

The negatives of Judaism were alien to Smart's way of thinking, but it seems also that there were things that his benevolence would not allow him to mention at all and they included murder, adultery, and theft. The Eighth Commandment is turned about completely, and, instead of simply being asked not to steal, we are urged to *distribute*, or, in the words of St Luke (18: 22), 'sell all that thou hast, and distribute unto the poor, and thou shalt have treasure in heaven'.

There is throughout these stanzas a generosity of spirit that shows us what Christianity ought to be. It is summed up in the one line 'Turn from old Adam to the New' (l. 280), which reminds us of the prayer pronounced over us at the time of our Baptism: 'O Merciful God, grant that the old Adam in this child may be so buried, that the new man may be raised up in him . . .'.

For Smart, none of the positives in this his new version of the decalogue can surpass the absolute imperative of *praise*. 'PRAISE above all – for praise prevails' (l. 295). For fifty stanzas he has sung the praise of David the praise-singer, but at this point comes a change in direction. David himself fades from the picture for a while and the emphasis is all on praise. There is in the three transitionary stanzas a subdued tone, providing an easing of the tempo and a moment of pause before the great paean of 'ADORATION' that is about to begin. 'For by the grace of God I am the Reviver of ADORATION amongst ENGLISH-MEN', he had announced in *Jubilate Agno* (B 332), and this word ADORATION, always in capitals, moves through each of the next twenty-one stanzas. At first it descends one line at a time, stanza by stanza, from the first line down to the last; this movement is then repeated, and finally 'ADORATION' holds its position in the first line of each of the remaining eight stanzas.

The section begins as 'an exercise upon the seasons', and nothing shows more clearly how far removed Smart was from that element of the Anglican Church that averted its eyes from the things of this world, and kept them firmly on the life-to-come. Smart adores the magnificence of the world he had so cruelly been shut away from, and he recreates it in his imagination. In his stanzas on spring there is an explosion of colour, life, and activity; there are green shoots, blossom, birds' eggs, and honey. The almonds are rich and the Ivis is gorgeous.

Summer is a time of paradisal peace. The winds and the waves are calm. These are halcyon days, both in the wild and at home. A man sits at his ease beneath a fig tree, his child at his feet, while the panther's 'playful cubs' go scampering about her. Autumn brings in a harvest of apples and nectarines, peaches and pomegranates, and even in winter, though the seas may freeze, there is still colour. 'The pheasant shows his pompous neck', and, as well as the laurel and the crocus, there is the 'chearful holly, pensive yew' and the 'holy thorn' of

Glastonbury. In these stanzas we see Smart the miniaturist at his most brilliant, his images shining with all the brightness and detail of the tiny vignettes that are sometimes found in the initials of illuminated manuscripts.

The sensuality of these stanzas leads us to the next section, which Smart calls 'an exercise on the senses and how to subdue them'. The first of the senses is touch, and a 'greedy damsel' is clearly in the wrong when she tries to 'clutch' a 'daring redbreast', while another bird, the bullfinch, delights us when it tries to 'catch the soft flute's iv'ry touch'.

It is not easy to understand exactly what Smart intends by the subduing of the senses. Clearly, the misuse of the sense of taste could lead to the deadly sin of gluttony, and, while we may be tempted by 'the luscious zest of fruit', God 'Commands desire be chaste' (l. 414). We are also told that 'he, who kneels and chants | Prevails his passions to controul' (ll. 382–3), but earlier we had been urged to 'Use all thy passions!' (l. 259). There seems to be some confusion over senses, passions and desires. A proper use of our passions and senses is probably what he is advocating: that we should use our eyes to look at the wonders of God's creation, and that we should listen to His word.

> Hark! 'tis a voice – how still, and small –
> That makes the cataracts to fall,
> Or bids the sea be smooth.
>
> (ll. 400–2)

But that sensible moderation, so favoured at the time, has no part whatsoever to play in the stanzas with which *A Song to David* begins to draw towards a close. It is now, in this final section, that David makes his triumphant return to the forefront of the poem. Smart calls it 'An amplification in five degrees', and tells us that it leads to the conclusion 'That the best poet which ever lived was thought worthy of the highest honour which possibly can be conceived, as *the Saviour of the world was ascribed to his house and called his son in the body.*' Taking five adjectives – sweet, strong, beauteous, precious, and glorious – he devotes three stanzas to each; the first two making a series of simple assertions: the sweetness of early morning dew on the leaves of the lime trees; the sweetness of the smile on the face of a young mother as she nurses her sleeping child. The third stanza then moves into a comparative degree and says that *sweeter* than all such things is the language of David's psalms.

And so it continues. Samson's riddle on the bees swarming inside the dead body of a lion – 'out of the strong came forth sweetness' – provides a link to the next three stanzas on strength. It is the strength of the entire animal world, in earth, air, and sea, that we are shown, and once again in a series of contrasts: the lion and the horse, the ostrich and the eagle, the swordfish and the whale. The animal world always provided Smart with the opportunity to exult in the exotic: *glede* will send most of us to our dictionaries to discover that it is the red kite, and even Smart thought it wise to add a footnote to tell us that *xiphias* is a swordfish.[24] Yet out of this abundance and complexity it is often his simplicity that comes as the greater surprise, and in stanza 72 it is not only that the 'man of pray'r' is stronger than any of these, but the reminder that, weak as we are, Christ has promised us, in the Sermon on the Mount, a place

> Where ask is have, where seek is find,
> Where knock is open wide.

(ll. 461–2)

With the end in sight now, the pace of the poem quickens and the verse gets louder: plosives replace sibilants, run-on lines appear, and the examples become so various we no longer know what to expect. Fleets are beautiful, armies are beautiful, and so are landscaped gardens, and so is the moon, and brides undressing on their wedding nights. Presented as a list like this, it sounds anarchic, but Smart weaves all his images together and one of the strongest unifying factors is alliteration – so often a device of bludgeoning obviousness – but one that in Smart's hands is seen to be capable of grace and subtlety.

> Beauteous the fleet before the gale;
> Beauteous the multitudes in mail,
>   Rank'd arms and crested heads:
> Beauteous the garden's umbrage mild,
> Walk, water, meditated wild,
>   And all the bloomy beds.

(ll. 463–8)

But the 'shepherd king upon his knees' is 'more beautiful', just as his heart, 'the Lord's own heart', is 'more precious', than the widow's mite, the flashing ruby, the cerulean pearl, the penitential tear, or Israel's feast of bowers.

Sweet, strong, beauteous, precious. These adjectives have resounded through twelve consecutive stanzas with instances and images from all over the world, but this is surpassed by three final stanzas where the things of this world are left behind and he reaches out for the heavens: the sun and the stars, the comets, the northern lights, and the last trump. They thunder and hosanna. Nine lines each begin with the great organ peal of 'Glorious'.

> Glorious the sun in mid career;
> Glorious th' assembled fires appear;
> Glorious the comet's train;
> Glorious the trumpet and alarm;
> Glorious th' almighty stretch'd-out arm;
> Glorious th' enraptur'd main:
>
> Glorious the northern lights astream;
> Glorious the song, when God's the theme;
> Glorious the thunder's roar:
> Glorious hosanna from the den;
> Glorious the catholic amen;
> Glorious the martyr's gore . . .

(ll. 499–510)

Even verbs are dispensed with in this final rush of glory. It is like the ending of a Handel chorus. It seems that it will never end. We do not really want it ever to end, but we reach a moment when we can take no more. And when it does end, it ends with what the poem and creation itself have all the time been heading towards: the coming of Christ, the son of David, the incarnation, and our salvation. *Consumatum est.* And when the great last line eventually does come, it is with one final triad of alliteration – those three massive chords in D

DETERMINED, DARED, and DONE.

(l. 516)

69

5

Hymns and Spiritual Songs

Jonathan Swift, though himself both a poet and a divine, held that religion was inimical to poetry: 'the smallest quantity of religion, like a single drop of Malt-Liquor in Claret, will muddy and discompose the brightest Poetical Genius.'[1] And by the time Samuel Johnson came to write his life of Isaac Watts, the matter seemed, to Johnson at least, to be quite settled. He tells his readers, 'his [Watts'] devotional poetry is, like that of others, unsatisfactory. The paucity of its topicks enforces perpetual repetition, and the sanctity of the matter rejects the ornaments of figurative diction. It is sufficient for Watts to have done better than others what no man has done well.'[2] Can Johnson or Swift ever have read Herbert?

This incompatibility between religion and poetry was argued from two differing angles. While some, like Swift and Johnson, believed that it was religion that was not a suitable subject for poetry, there were others who held that poetry was not a suitable vehicle for religion. What they questioned was its propriety, and in this they followed Calvin in his insistence that only the words of God Himself were fit to be used in the divine service. This meant an almost exclusive concentration on the Psalms, which he believed to have been expressly dictated from heaven. Luther, who saw nothing wrong with singing German folk songs over a jug of beer, was not so afraid of the arts. He wrote hymns that spread all over Europe, until the priests complained that he was singing the people into Protestantism.[3] The Church of England fought shy of such things and remained very much a psalm-singing church. Even in the middle of the nineteenth century George Eliot could write of Shepperton, 'The innovation of hymn books was as yet undreamed of.'[4]

It was among the Dissenters that the tradition of hymn singing was first established in this country, due in part to their greater personal freedom of worship and as a reaction against a time when the only singing in church was by the priests, or a choir trained by priests, and was in Latin. But even Isaac Watts, our first great hymn-writer, and a Dissenter by birth, had to struggle to have his ideas accepted. In his *Preface to Horae Lyricae* he wrote, 'some weaker Christians ... imagine that poetry and vice are akin, or at least that verse is fit only to recommend trifles and entertain our looser hours ...'.[5] However, he won the struggle. His success was outstanding and he went on to produce some of the most famous and best-loved hymns in the language: among them being 'When I survey the wond'rous cross', 'Jesus shall reign where'er the sun', and 'Our God, our help in ages past'.

If we were to analyse 'Our God, our help in ages past' and ask what makes it such a fine hymn, we would realize first that it is eminently singable.

> Our God, our help in ages past,
> Our hope for years to come,
> Our shelter from the stormy blast,
> And our eternal home.

The regularity of the common metre ensures that there will be no wobbles, elisions, or uncertainties. There are no hard words to puzzle and make us stumble. The language is plain, the syntax straightforward, and each line is a self-contained unit, so that it could be 'lined-out' if need be without any hiatus in the sense. There is a certain fervour to it and it also has the merit of being not too long.

If regularity, simplicity, and universality are three features that would seem to be essential for a good hymn, when we turn to Smart it is not long before we realize that all too often he fails on each score. He even fails on the question of length. His 'Easter Day' extends to 128 lines. Thirty-two verses. No congregation could cope with that. And it is not an isolated instance. 'The King's Restoration' has 120 lines, and these are even longer, the final one in each of its twenty elaborate stanzas running to twelve syllables.

When it suited him Smart could write with great simplicity, but his hymn on 'The Trinity', even when read on the page, is complex on a theological level alone. His range of reference is uncompromising, not to say eccentric, requiring, and indeed acquiring, footnotes at times to identify the biblical references. In Hymn II it is a knowledge of Pliny that is needed, and 'The King's Restoration' includes a mention of one David Gam (even Smart gets this wrong and spells it 'Cam'), a soldier who fought at Agincourt.

It is a sequence that, judged as a collection of hymns, would have to be said to be an almost total failure, but they are not hymns as we understand the word. Even when Smart entitled his sequence *Hymns and Spiritual Songs for the Fasts and Festivals of the Church of England*, he was not announcing that it was intended to be used as a hymnbook. The words come from Paul's Epistle to the Ephesians 5: 18–19, 'be filled with the Spirit. Speaking to yourselves in psalms and hymns and spiritual songs, singing and making melody in your heart to the Lord.' Paul's words suggest not a church service but a private act of worship.

The complexity of the overall structure of the sequence is itself enough to mark it out as not being a collection of hymns as we would understand the word. As a sequence it forms a circle, and each hymn within that circle is linked to the one that follows it, as in Donne's *La Corona*, by the rhetorical device known as *concatenatio*. Sometimes the link is formed by the repetition of single words, as between 'Circumcision' and 'Epiphany':

> 'This is my HEIR of GRACE,
>   'In whose perfections I rejoice.'
> GRACE, thou source of each perfection.

Or by association of ideas:

> Remember Peter's tears.
>
>   'Ash Wednesday'
>
> HARK! the cock proclaims the morning,
>
>   'St Matthias'

Or by the negation of an idea:

Misers have no hope.

'St Barnabas'

GREAT and bounteous BENEFACTOR,

'The Nativity of St John the Baptist'

There is nothing mechanical about this device. Smart accomplishes it with variety and wit and when the last line of the sequence is reached, 'In the worship of the WORD', we are sent back to the opening line of the first hymn, 'WORD of endless adoration'. The circle of the church year is thus complete and truly endless.

A further link is also established within the circle of the year by reference to animals, birds, and flowers that are appropriate to each of the seasons. In the first three hymns winter is giving way to spring, and the pansy, the lily of the valley, and the 'Brousing kids, and lambkins grazing' (III, l. 45) replace the evergreens and myrtles (I, l. 25). 'St Mark' (25 April) begins 'PULL up the bell-flow'rs of the spring, | And let the budding greenwood ring', and on the first of May ('St Philip and St James') the verses blossom with 'tansy, calaminth and daisies', 'couslips' (*sic*) and 'corn-flow'rs'; there are bluecaps and blackbirds singing, and goldfinches among the thistles. In Hymns XVIII and XIX we hear of the swelling fruits of summer, the waving of the corn, and the larks on their nests. 'St Simon and St Jude' (28 October) has references to the goodly crop and the decoration of the church for Harvest Festival, and finally by Christmas Day the snow has returned, 'Nature's decorations glisten', and the Glastonbury Thorn is in flower.

This cycle of the natural world would be meaningful to a congregation; they would have heard these birds and seen these flowers on their way to and from the church. The same cannot, however, be said of the *concatenatio*, when there is sometimes a gap of weeks between one hymn and its neighbour. This is a device not of a hymn-writer, but of a poet. As a hymn-writer Smart is probably a failure, but read these hymns as *poems* and it is soon evident that he is one of the few truly great religious poets since the days of Herbert, Crashaw, and Traherne.

* * *

73

In establishing how Smart went about constructing this sequence much has been made of his dependence on Robert Nelson's *A Companion for the Festivals and Fasts of the Church of England with Collects and Prayers for each Solemnity*, in which the historical and spiritual significance of each of the festivals and fasts is explained through a series of questions and answers. Nelson himself was not a churchman, but his learned and authoritative book, first published in 1704, was widely read; it had gone into twenty-one editions by 1757 and was still being printed well into the next century.

The chief advocate of Smart's dependence on Nelson is Moira Dearnley in her book *The Poetry of Christopher Smart*, where fifteen pages are devoted to establishing the connections.[6] Smart's editors have accepted her argument (*PW* ii. 7), but a close look at the evidence shows it to be somewhat flawed. Referring to Smart's second hymn, 'Circumcision', Dearnley says that, 'There are remarkable parallels between the theological statements made by Nelson and Smart respectively.'[7] She cites Nelson's question, 'What rite of Admission into the Christian Church answered to that of Circumcision under the Law?' and his answer: 'The Sacrament of Baptism'. She then misreads Nelson's biblical authority for this as Colossians 3: 11–12, and says that it contains 'after all no direct reference to Baptism', whereas Nelson's authority is actually Colossians 2: 11–12, which clearly does. Wrongly attributing the connection to Nelson himself, she then concludes that 'Nelson's esoteric point is nevertheless taken up by Smart'. Of course the point is not esoteric at all, but a standard interpretation, and features as such in Isaac Watts's hymn 'Circumcision and Baptism'. She detects a further link in Nelson's statement that circumcision figuratively represents 'That as our Birth is impure by Reason of Original Sin, so we ought to lay aside all Filthiness and superfluity of Naughtiness, putting off the Body of the Sins of the Flesh' and points to Smart's fifth stanza, but she has not seen that part of the Collect for the day reads, 'Grant us the true circumcision of the Spirit, that our hearts and all our members being mortified from all worldly and carnal lusts, we may in all things obey thy blessed will.' The similarities between Smart and Nelson are there because they are both following traditional teaching and both are reading their Bible and their Book of Common Prayer. Nothing in Smart's hymn is proof that he was working from Nelson. The evidence shows instead how indebted he was to his prayer book. In Hymn XXVII, 'St Simon and St Jude', Smart wrote:

> He his pilgrimage perform'd
> Far as the Britannic coast,
> And the ready converts swarm'd
> To receive the Holy Ghost.
>
> (ll. 13–16)

Mrs Dearnley points out that Nelson had written, 'He is said also to have passed into Britain . . .'. But the Book of Common Prayer current in Smart's day (I have an edition dated 1749) contains sixty-four illustrated plates representing incidents from the life of Christ or a portrait of the saints; each has a caption and that for St Simon reads, 'He preached in Egypt, Africa, and Britain, and at length was crucified.'

Similarly, she refers to Nelson's statement that St Andrew 'came at last to Petrea in Achaia', but, when Smart writes 'His body was remov'd | From Petrae to the Turk', he is following the spelling in the caption to the portrait of the saint, 'He was fastened to a cross at Patrae in Achaia from which he preached several days.'

As we have already seen that it was from his prayer book that Smart worked throughout his translation of the psalms, it is only to be expected that this also would be his chief source for the hymns.

Four of Smart's hymns have no counterparts in Nelson because they are occasioned by neither festivals nor fasts, but were what were known as 'Solemn Days', celebrating the Martyrdom of the Blessed King Charles the First (30 January), the King's Restoration (29 May), the Accession of the Ruling Monarch (25 October), and the Most Traiterous and bloody intended Massacre by Gunpowder (5 November).[8]

The opening line of 'King Charles the Martyr', 'The persecutor was redeem'd', is the link that joins it to the previous hymn, 'Conversion of Saint Paul'. It was in the writings of St Paul, as Smart explains, that the extremists among the seventeenth-century Puritan movement found those texts that they would assiduously twist and distort to justify some new sect or schism, and these were the persecutors who brought about the downfall – the martyrdom – of the King.

Woven into what could be seen as a personal historical view are strands of biblical authority. Line 7, 'All against Christ alike', picks up a theme from the Order of Morning Service for the day, which begins with an antiphon composed of verses from the Psalms, with the priest reciting Psalm 2: 2, 'The people stood up, and the rulers took counsel together: against the Lord, and against his anointed.' This parallel between the martyrdom of Christ and of Charles is further justified by the Second Lesson for the day, Matthew 27, describing how Christ was spat upon and the rending of the veil in the temple.

> When Christ was spitted on and slain,
> The temple rent her veil in twain;
> And in the hour that Charles was cast
> The church had well nigh groan'd its last.
>
> (ll. 17–20)

Smart is following the traditions and conventions of the time, but there are also certain idiosyncrasies of his own. One is his intense patriotism, which leads him to see the English as God's own chosen people, 'the land of God's selected sheep' (l. 11), a belief he had put forward in *Jubilate Agno*: 'For the ENGLISH are the seed of Abraham' (B 433). Another is his intense hostility to the Church of Rome. The Puritans, as Smart saw it, were not Charles's only trouble.

> Ah great unfortunate, the chief
> Of monarchs in the tale of grief,
> By marriage ill-advis'd, akin
> To Moab and the man of sin!
>
> (ll. 13–16)

Charles had the great misfortune to have married a Roman Catholic, Henrietta Maria, sister of Louis XIII, the man of sin. Smart knew just what a disaster this could be as he himself had a Catholic wife, Anna Maria Carnan, who had helped bring about his martyrdom in the madhouse, and in *Jubilate Agno* she too is a 'Moabitish woman' (B 56). He could therefore feel doubly and personally sorry for Charles I.

Smart's hostility towards Roman Catholics is expressed in far more forceful terms elsewhere in this sequence. In his Hymn on 'The Fifth of November' we read:

> This was deem'd a fit occasion
>   For the Papists to be bold,
> For the children of evasion
>   To come sneaking from their hold.
>
> What a plan of devastation,
>   That the dev'l alone could start,

(ll. 13–18)

However our sensibilities may react to such sentiments today, it seems pointless to criticize or to blame Smart. They were the sentiments of his time. Roman Catholics were the enemy. It has to be remembered that it was once an effigy of the Pope, not of Guy Fawkes, that the people of England used to burn on 5 November. We think of Andrew Marvell as being an urbane and civilized man, but he considered that *'Popery* is such a thing as cannot . . . be called a *Religion'*.[9] The inscription on the Monument to the Great Fire of London still attributed it to the 'Treacheries and Malice of the Popish Faction' until 1831, and the brutalities of the Gordon riots took place only nine years after Smart's death.

Hostility to Rome was not simply acceptable; it was expected. In 1764 when Smart published his 'Ode to the Right Honourable the Earl of Northumberland' and spent almost a quarter of the poem attacking Rome, the *Monthly Review* praised him for that specifically: 'he merits the thanks of every true Protestant, for he fights with a truly British spirit against the Whore of Babylon.'[10]

Hymn XVII, 'The King's Restoration', celebrates another of the 'Solemn Days'. Such a tribute to the House of Stuart may seem a touch wayward in Hanovarian England, with the Papist Young Pretender still alive and living in Rome, but it was a festival that continued to be recognized by the Church. Although Smart blesses the Stuarts twice in *Jubilate Agno*, he was no rebel, as we can see from his hymn on 'The Accession of King George III'. His benevolent nature would have led him to bless anyone who was afflicted. In any case, the only direct reference to Charles II comes at the end of this long poem and it is clear that Smart is more concerned with the restoration and triumph of the Church of England than with any dynastic party politics. This is the theme of the First Collect of the Day, which celebrates the fact that the Restoration 'didst restore also unto us the publick and free Profession of thy true Religion and Worship'.

The particular aspect of the service Smart chose to concentrate on in his own hymn is that of 'remembrance'. The first response of the people in the opening antiphon is from Psalm 111: 4, 'The merciful and gracious Lord hath so done his marvellous works: that they ought to be had in remembrance'. *Remember* was also one of the last words spoken by Charles on the scaffold, and the call to *remember* is sounded six times in the closing four stanzas.

These *remembrances* might, at first reading, seem little more than a rather rambling history lesson. An invocation is followed by a sequence of five stanzas each beginning 'We thank thee . . .' and which give thanks to God, first for the overall excellence of the British people, then for the River Thames, and for St Paul's Cathedral, from where 'George's gallant horse' had lately ridden off to engage the French, 'Moab's spurious seed', in the Seven Years War. But the main thrust of these stanzas is the thanks Smart offers up for the British navy. It is hard to explain the passion Smart had for the navy, but passion it was.

> We thank thee for the naval sway
> Which o'er the subject seas we claim;
> And for the homage nations pay,
> Submissive to the great Britannic fame;
> Who soon as they thy precious cross discern,
> Bow lowering to the staff on our imperial stern.

(ll. 19–24)

There is something actual and vivid about that white ensign.

Then we go back to Elizabethan times, but still with the navy, to 'Howard, Frobisher, and glorious Drake', who together had defeated the Armada. After that it is the eighteenth century again, when three British vessels, 'mann'd from heav'n' but captained by Forest, Suckling, and Langdon, had seen off a squadron of seven French ships at the battle of Cape François.

Next come five stanzas beginning 'The glory to thy name . . .' and they take us even further back in time to the victories 'At Poictier's and in Cressey's field'.

Three stanzas then praise Queen Anne for the churches she built, and her bounty in providing for poor clergy and finally her admirals, 'Russel, Shovel, Rook, a Benbow, and a Byng'. These jumps in time are unpredictable; the building of churches and the sinking of ships seem unrelated, but the structure of the poem and especially the discipline of the stanza form not only hold it all together; they are suggestive of method and system, and, if we look back to the invocation, we can see the line of thought Smart was following. Christ is

> The sole original and cause
> Of all heroic actions past,
> The God of patriot deeds . . .
>
> (ll. 2–4)

And all the people mentioned in this poem – the recent and the historical – have this in common, that they are heroes and patriots, but heroes and patriots *in the cause of the Lord*.

At line 85 the poem at last turns to the Restoration and to Charles. We are given a rousing picture of the celebrations held on what had become known as Oak-Apple Day on account of his hiding place after the Battle of Worcester:

> Remember all the pious vows
>   Made by our ancestors, for us,
> That we should thus dispose the boughs,
>   And wear the royal oak in triumph thus;
> And to the skies, the caps of freedom hurl'd,
> Should thus proclaim the queen of islands and the world.
>
> (ll. 103–8)

Eventually something had to be said in favour of Charles himself. The difficulty of the task seems to be acknowledged in the image 'Select the nosegay from the sod; | But leave the brambles in the wood.' All the brambles of Charles's extravagances are ignored and Smart selects the nosegay of the building of the Chelsea Hospital and the Hospital at Greenwich for those 'remov'd from seaman's toils'. Both were homes for heroes and so this is perfectly in keeping with the dominant theme of the poem.

The importance to Smart of this concept of the Christian Hero can be seen in the secular odes that he published in 1763, one 'To Admiral Sir George Pocock' (written in the same unusual stanza form as the 'Restoration' hymn) and one 'To General Draper'. Both men had had considerable campaign success. Draper, a contemporary of Smart's at Cambridge, and twice mentioned in *Jubilate Agno*, had commanded the expedition that captured Manila in 1762, and Pocock had captured Havana in the same year. Neither, in Smart's view, had received the public recognition he deserved (nor had he), but each had received something of far greater value: they had received what Smart called 'God's applause' and this is central to both poems.

But Christian heroes are not the same as saints. Sainthood is a concept that the Church of England has never felt fully at ease with. There is something dangerously Romish about saints. One of the Articles of Religion asserts that 'The Romish doctrine concerning . . . Invocation of Saints, is a fond thing vainly invented, and grounded upon no warranty of Scripture, but rather repugnant to the Word of God.' Smart had already been gently taken to task by the *Critical Review* in its notice of *A Song to David* – 'Without venturing to criticize on the propriety of a Protestant's offering up either hymns or prayers to the dead . . .'[11] – and there is no hint whatsoever of idolatry in these hymns. Instead he goes out of his way in 'St Luke' to castigate icons, statuary, and the like. They are called 'detested arts'. Luke had been credited with having painted a picture of the Virgin Mary, and, while that in itself was not wrong, it had seemingly led to the most terrible consequences:

> Her the hypocrites adore
> In the fane of modern Rome,
> And from the shadows aid implore,
> That they may blaspheme the more,
> And the more presume.

(ll. 31–5)

If there is no hint of idolatry, neither are there any invocations, or suggestions that the saints might have been assigned any special tasks such as watching over particular groups or looking out for lost causes, or helping to find lost things. Smart's saints are a robust and practical group of men, of 'manly vigour' (XIX, l. 43), whose God is a God 'of heartiness and strength' (XXI, l. 43), and what seems to have interested him most is what they achieved in their lives and how they died; in other words, how they attained their status as Christian Heroes.

The opening to 'St James' might provide a clue to Smart's veneration for the navy, as James, the fisherman, was mending his nets by the sea of Galilee when Christ called him to become a fisher of men.

> Sure a seaman's lot is bless'd,
>   Gen'rous, faithful, frank, and brave,
> Since the Lord himself possess'd
>   Of disciples from the wave.
> Sure a realm, whose fame depends
> On their deeds the rest transcends.
>
> (ll. 1–6)

And the rather idealistic equation looks to be that, as the British navy extended the Empire around the world, so the word of God went with them, and all sailors become evangelists and thereby heroes. James, through his association with Santiago de Compostela, is pre-eminent as the pilgrim saint and in this hymn God is asked to 'Prosper thou the pilgrim sent | To prepare the great event.'

As well as being evangelists, the saints were also called upon to become martyrs. In 'St Matthias' we read:

> Hard and precious are together,
>   Stripes and wounds are endless gain;
> If with him the storm we weather,
>   With him also we shall reign.
>
> (ll. 33–6)

They gave up their lives, but first, like St Barnabas, they gave up all their worldly possessions.

> Heroes of the Christian cause,
> Candidates for God's applause,
>   – Leaving all for Christ his sake . . .
>
> (ll. 19–21)

Smart himself was never over-encumbered by worldly possessions or treasure upon earth for moth and rust to corrupt, so this rejection of material things may seem rather an empty convention on his part, but what is important to recognize is that, while rejecting materialism, he is not rejecting the material world and in this he is very far removed from other hymn-writers of his day, especially the evangelicals.

Although Watts was sometimes capable of a Smart-like recognition that the created world praises God by the very fact of its existence, what we hear more frequently in his hymns is a tone of world-weariness: there is nothing here, it seems, to detain him, and his sight is set on those joys that are to be found only in the afterlife.

> There's nothing round this spacious earth
> That suits my large desire;
> To boundless joy and solid mirth
> My nobler thoughts aspire.[12]

It is not only the created physical world that Watts sees as getting in the way of such joys; he even rejects the love of family and friends in a hymn entitled 'Love to the Creatures Dangerous'.

> Our dearest joys, and nearest friends,
> The partners of our blood,
> How they divide our wavering minds,
> And leave but half to God.[13]

A sentiment as life-denying as this seems so unnatural that it is hard to believe that it was meant seriously. It seems more in the nature of pious posturing, but it is not the only unhealthy element in Watts, for, while we are persuaded to accept death as something to long for, being our doorway to heaven, he can be found dwelling on the physical facts of it in macabre and grisly detail.

> His quiv'ring lip hangs feebly down,
> His pulses faint and few;
> Then speechless, with a doleful groan
> He bids the world adieu.[14]

Smart's hymns, being celebrations of the liturgical calendar, would not have lent themselves so readily to such things, but we can sense instantly that such an approach to the world, to life, and to death would have been totally foreign to him. It is his absolute joy in the world that he sings. He is a praise-singer and the 'Reviver of ADORATION amongst ENGLISH-MEN' (*JA* B 332)

Even in his hymn on 'The Crucifixion of Our Blessed Lord', it is the miracles that Christ performed during his life rather than the agony of his death Smart concentrates on, and there is none of that Evangelical preoccupation with blood. We never hear him beating his breast, as Charles Wesley does – 'I am all unclean, unclean' – nor is there any of that taut anguish of introspection and doubt there is in Cowper.

Smart was secure in his faith. There is never a trace of doubt, and for all his suffering there is no dwelling on the miseries of the world. Because of the nature of the task he set himself, the autobiographical element in his hymns is far less evident than in those of Wesley and Cowper, but it is there, and at an early stage, in the hymn on the 'Epiphany', where he considers the gifts that he has to offer to Christ. The Magi had been wise men from the east who had travelled following the star to Bethlehem. Smart is a 'western palmer', but, confined as he is, he cannot travel anywhere, at least not physically. But, following the star of divine grace, when he goes down on his knees he can travel in spirit. His nephew, Christopher Hunter, wrote that 'Mr Smart, in composing the religious poems, was frequently so impressed with the sentiment of devotion, as to write particular passages on his knees'.[15] 'Lo! I travel in the spirit, | On my knees my course I steer' ('Epiphany', ll. 9–10). He has no purse or scrip to carry like a real pilgrim, but he has his Bible and his prayer book. He is certainly as poor as any of the apostles and he knows only too well that he has no rich gifts to offer, but he can offer 'strains of love'. He can and will offer up his verses, which, though he is alone and living 'Midst unnumber'd ills', will nevertheless express his gratitude for God's bounty. He will also take it upon himself to express the gratitude of all God's mute creation.

Smart's most famous expression of this theme is in his hymn on 'The Presentation of Christ in the Temple'.

> I speak for all – for them that fly,
> And for the race that swim;

> For all that dwell in moist and dry,
> Beasts, reptiles, flow'rs and gems to vie
> When gratitude begins her hymn.

(ll. 41–5)

Not untypically he avoids the central issue of the festival almost entirely in this hymn and it would seem to have been the idea of the temple itself that first appealed to the Freemason in him. He begins with the building of it from David's plan. It was a magnificent structure capable of accommodating a vast congregation, yet it was not big enough, Smart tells us, to accommodate God himself. That could be achieved only when the Old Covenant of the Law, represented here by Solomon's temple, had been replaced by the New Covenant: the temple of Christ's body and thus the establishment of the Christian Church. As St John had put it, 'he spake of the temple of his body' (2: 21). And this is the miracle of the Incarnation: that, while Solomon's temple was not vast enough to contain the immensity of the Godhead, he came to us himself in the body of a child.

This replacement of the Old Covenant by the New is a belief that shaped much of Smart's thinking. It was behind his translation of the Psalms, where 'All things that seem contrary to Christ are omitted, and evangelical matter put in their room.' His whole concept of gratitude is based on his insistence that there are two things for which we should be eternally grateful: the Creation and the Incarnation.

He saw it as his duty as a Christian poet to speak for all creation and at this point in the hymn he gives up any pretence that it may be dealing with the presentation of Christ in the temple. Instead he takes off into one of his great choruses of praise. Following the order in which he had stated his theme in the stanza just quoted, he celebrates it in six brilliant miniatures.

> Praise him ye doves, and ye that pipe
> Ere buds begin to stir;
> Ev'n every finch of every stripe,
> And thou of filial love the type,
> O stork! that sit'st upon the fir.

Praise him thou sea, to whom he gave
   The shoal of active mutes;
(Fit tenants of thy roaring wave)
Who comes to still the fiends, that rave
   In oracles and school disputes.

By Jesus number'd all and priz'd,
   Praise him in dale and hill;
Ye beasts for use and peace devis'd,
And thou which patient and despis'd,
   Yet shalt a prophecy fulfill.

Praise him ye family that weave
   The crimson to be spread
There, where communicants receive,
And ye, that form'd the eye to grieve,
   Hid in green bush or wat'ry bed.

Praise him ye flow'rs that serve the swarm
   With honey for their cells;
Ere yet the vernal day is warm,
To call out millions to perform
   Their gambols on your cups and bells.

Praise him ye gems of lively spark,
   And thou the pearl of price;
In that great depth or caverns dark,
Nor yet are wrested from the mark,
   To serve the turns of pride and vice.

(ll. 46–75)

Like all great miniatures, the closer one looks at them the more one is surprised and enchanted by the detail. There is the precise painterly 'finch of every stripe' and the ironic suggestion that the mute fish is the best tenant of the roaring wave, but these stanzas are also filled with biblical echoes that pick out the spiritual history of man from the Fall to the Saving Grace. The dove could be Noah's bird of hope, but it was also, as the Gospel for the day (Luke 2: 22–40) tells us, a designated part of the temple sacrifice when Christ was presented. The beast that would fulfil a prophecy ('patient and despis'd' is equally an echo of Isaiah 53: 3; 'he was despised and rejected of man') is the ass on which Jesus rode into Jerusalem. The reptile that 'form'd the eye to grieve' is the serpent (Gen. 3: 5) that opened the eyes of Adam and Eve to grief. The pearl of great price is the kingdom of heaven (Matt. 13: 45–6) and a symbol of our salvation. And the poem ends with that unique creature the phoenix, which rises again from its own ashes and is a symbol of the Resurrection.

Smart could stay close to the concerns of a particular festival if he chose, and he chose to when writing 'The Conversion of St Paul'. It is a compact and complex poem, beginning not with Paul but with three stanzas that recount nine Old Testament miracles: Joshua causing the sun to stand still at the Battle of Gibeon (Josh. 10: 112–13); God's reversal of the progress of the sun as a sign to Hezekiah (Isa. 38: 8); the birth of a son to Hannah (1 Sam. 1); the widow's son brought back to life by Elijah (1 Kgs. 17: 17–23); Naaman being cured of leprosy (2 Kgs. 5: 1–14); the filling of a cruse of oil (1 Kgs. 17: 12–16); the iron axe head that floated (2 Kgs. 6: 5–6); the parting of the waters of the Red Sea (Exod. 14: 15–30); and of those of the River Jordan (Josh. 3: 15–17). These were all miracles that, as the fourth stanza says, 'in ancient days occurr'd'. Smart chooses to see them as being surpassed by the miracles of the New Testament and shows how each of them pales by comparison with the conversion of St Paul. Again he does so in three stanzas. The sun may recede, but that was nothing to making such 'a profligate recede'. The calming of his madness was more remarkable than the calming of those waters. Iron may have floated, but his steel heart was softened and the filling of his heart with grace was greater than the filling of a cruse with oil. His 'internal blackness' was a sickness worse than leprosy and his soul was worse than dead, yet how miraculous it was that spiritual barrenness should bear such fruit.

The last stanza is then balanced against the fourth, where the miracles of those 'ancient days' are contrasted with the conversion of Paul, who is described as being 'a servant of the times', and thus we are presented with a poem whose structure seems a minor miracle in itself.

There is a far stronger homiletic strain in Wesley and Watts than is ever found in Smart and this is to be expected; they were both leaders of new movements within the Church and had new ideas and new doctrines to advocate, whereas Smart stood faithful to the Anglican tradition. This is very evident in his hymn on 'Trinity Sunday'. No doctrine has occasioned more debate than that of the Trinity, but Smart's position, if not anti-intellectual, is opposed to the need for any debate at all. He dismisses all the 'books, that load the shelves, | to lead us from ourselves'. To him, the Trinity as propounded in the Athanasian Creed – 'the whole three Persons are co-eternal together: and co-equal' – is a simple truth. In 1 John 5: 7, the Second Lesson for evensong on Trinity Sunday, it says 'For there are three that bear record in heaven, the Father, the Word, and the Holy Ghost: and these three are one.' And Smart accepts this without question: 'Yet all the Scriptures run | That God is great and one.' And he adds to this the authority of the Psalms. 'The Trinity is plain, | So David's psalms maintain.'

And his confidence in the simplicity of this doctrine of the Trinity allows him to weave in and out of the poem patterns of the numbers three and one. Each of its ten $(3 \times 3 + 1)$ stanzas has six lines and each of the first four is a trimeter, and in addition to this he included six of his favourite device – the triad: for example, 'By submission, pray'r and praise', and 'One lord, one faith, one font'. Of these triads, the most interesting is 'Man, soul and angel', which had also appeared in the *Song*, where David is described as 'Man, soul, and angel, without peer'. In Genesis 1: 26 God had said, 'Let us make man in our own image, after our likeness', the use of the plural implying the Trinity, and so, if man is made in the image of God, then he must possess within him a trinity analogous to the Holy Trinity. Man is our mortal nature. Soul is that part of us that is immortal and we also, in Smart's view, have a guardian angel. In 'St Michael and All Angels' he tells us:

> These, one for every man, are sent
>   God in the spirit to reveal,
> To forward ev'ry good event,
>   And each internal grief to heal.

(ll. 33–6)

These angels not only protect us, they guide us. In the *Song* we are told of David ' 'Twas he the famous temple plann'd: | (The seraph in his soul)'. And it must have been the seraph in his own soul that brought into being the finest of these poems.

87

Few lyric poets have managed to depict the English rural scene with a brightness to equal that of Smart, and this is especially true of Hymn XIII, 'St Philip and St James', whose festival falls on May Day. The first eleven stanzas of this poem are a sensuous celebration of spring.

> Muse, accordant to the season,
> Give the numbers life and air . . .

(ll. 9–10)

he had prayed and there is life in abundance here.

It is not just a static description. There is movement too. Even the perfume of the flowers is blown towards us on the breeze. The stream 'leaps alive'; the 'couslips' 'seize' upon the fallow. There are things to smell, to see, and to hear.

> Hark! aloud, the black-bird whistles,
> With surrounding fragrance blest,
> And the goldfinch in the thistles
> Makes provision for her nest.

(ll. 37–40)

There is an actuality in Smart's choice of flowers. They are not the commonplaces of the pastoral, but 'Tansy, calaminth and daisies'. He knows what he is writing about: lady's smock is given its more exact botanical name Cardamine.

The language is alive too. The biblical reference to the lilies of the field becomes 'And the lily smiles supremely | Mention'd by the Lord on earth.' The luxuriance of 'supremely' is followed by the matter-of-fact 'Mention'd', as though the lilies are alive to the honour that has been done them and regard the slightest mention of them by our Lord as putting them a cut above all other flowers.

Philip and James eventually make their appearance in the poem by way of contrast. The goldfinch and the blackbird have nests; the hornet has a hive and the coney has rocks for its fortress-home, but the saints have no such security or comfort.

> But the servants of their Saviour,
> Which with gospel-peace are shod,
> Have no bed but what the paviour
> Makes them in the porch of God.

(ll. 45–8)

Their lot is to be Christian heroes and martyrs, 'Born to weep, to starve and die!' And that is why their song is to be sung this day in the house of God. They were called upon to follow in their master's footsteps and to die for him. Their Saviour's final hour is recalled when he

> Who, for cruel traitors pleading,
>   Triumph'd in his parting breath;
> O'er all miracles preceding
>   His inestimable death.

(ll. 73–6)

Among so much life his death is inestimable and the breath with which the poem had begun, 'the breath upon the bloom', is now his 'parting breath'.

Much of the poem's success derives from the lightness of tone that comes as a result of its trochaic metre, where the rich feminine rhymes of the eight-syllable first and third lines are followed by masculine rhymes in the second and fourth, which have only seven syllables. Thus each quatrain ends with a very distinctive 'upbeat', which accounts for the overall air of cheerfulness.

This same metre is employed in Hymn XXXII, 'The Nativity of Our Lord and Saviour Jesus Christ', and helps to give it too an air of exuberance. It opens with some urgency

> Where is this stupendous stranger,
>   Swains of Solyma, advise,
> Lead me to my Master's manger,
>   Shew me where my Saviour lies?

(ll. 1–4)

Smart cannot wait to behold this miracle. The grandeur of it is in the Latinate grandeur of the language. But the real miracle of it is that God has become a child and not only a child but a child that is 'mean and lowly', so the magnificence is blended with simplicity in a telling sequence of paradoxes.

> O the magnitude of meekness!
>   Worth from worth immortal sprung;
> O the strength of infant weakness,
>   If eternal is so young!

(ll. 9–12)

Because of this birth the 'pow'rs of darkness (are) routed' and in the natural world this is marked by yet further paradoxes. Boreas, the cold north wind, is calmed; the box and the laurel, evergreens and so symbols of eternity, glisten with frost and snow. It is as if everything is sharing in this birth and coming to life.

> For before the NATIVITY is the dead of the winter and after it the quick.
>
> (JA B 305)

The birds acknowledge it and sing in a stanza that itself sings unforgettably through our minds.

> Spinks and ouzels sing sublimely,
> 'We too have a Saviour born;'
> Whiter blossoms burst untimely
> On the blest Mosaic thorn.
>
> (ll. 29–32)

The 'Mosaic thorn' Smart mentions is partly the rod of Aaron, which bloomed when Moses laid it in the tabernacle (Num. 17), but more specifically it is the Holy Thorn of Glastonbury (see also JA B 232), which grew from the staff of Joseph of Arimathea, and which still flowers, as I was once told by a gardener there, on Christmas Day, *Old Style*.

The Incarnation and the Creation, which are at the centre of so much of Smart's religious thinking, are then linked together, bringing this astonishing Christmas hymn to a close with a statement that jolts us with its simplicity.

> God all-bounteous, all-creative,
> Whom no ills from good dissuade,
> Is incarnate, and a native
> Of the very world he made.
>
> (ll. 33–6)

6

Hymns for the Amusement of Children

It can sometimes seem as if childhood was not invented until the second half of the eighteenth century. In family portraits such as Hogarth's painting of the MacKinnon children in 1742, it is not only the adult-looking clothes we notice, it is also a worldly, knowing look about their eyes. These children are miniatures of their parents. A century later, however, and we have the other extreme in George Richmond's mawkish painting of Swinburne and his sisters. All three are dressed as girls, and Richmond has worked so hard to capture what was then felt to be *innocence* that the eyes are empty, the faces pallid and insipid. Similarly, when we go back to what is perhaps the first book of poetry written especially for children – John Bunyan's *A Book for Boys and Girls: Or Country Rhymes for Children*, published in 1686 – we find a tone that is forbiddingly moral. Here nothing is innocent. Nothing is to be enjoyed. These poems may be intended for children, but any mention of a childish activity – chasing a butterfly, or whipping a top – is occasion for a terrible warning and they provide an ample demonstration of the mind-forged manacles and repressions that Blake was to struggle against in his *Songs of Innocence and Experience*.

Bunyan, however, was not as fierce as many of his co-religionists. To the Calvinists children were not innocent. They were fallen creatures, damned by the sin of Adam from the moment of their birth and in dire need of salvation at no matter what mental or bodily cost. Susanna Wesley, the mother of John and Charles, was uncompromising on this score.

This, therefore, I cannot but earnestly repeat, -Break their wills betimes; begin this great work before they can run alone, before they can speak plain, or perhaps speak at all ... Let a child, from a year old, be taught to fear the rod and to cry softly.[1]

The logic is faultless. If children were really such miserable little sinners, then clearly no parent could risk indulging their childish ways. Children had to obey and if they did not, then the consequences, according to Isaac Watts, would be disastrous.

> Have you not heard what dreadful Plagues
>   Are threaten'd by the LORD,
> To him that breaks his Father's law,
>   Or mocks his Mother's Word?
>
> What heavy guilt upon him lies!
>   How cursed is his Name!
> The Ravens shall pick out his Eyes,
>   And Eagles eat the same.[2]

Watts had expressed the hope that these songs of his would give children 'something to think upon when alone'.[3]

Watts's *Divine Songs Attempted in Easy Language for the Use of Children* (1715) was the most famous collection of poems for children to be published in the century and the various parodies it was subjected to – especially those of Lewis Carrol – are testimony to the longevity of its influence. His songs do run in the mind, but the overall impression they leave is of death, sin, and the fear of Hell.

> There is an Hour when I must die,
>   Nor do I know how soon 'twill come;
> A thousand children young as I,
>   Are call'd by Death to hear their Doom.[4]

Once having established in the minds of his young readers a very clear notion of Hell, he tells them what they must do to avoid going there, or rather what they must not do, as, predictably enough, his advice consists of a series of proscriptions, warning them against lying, quarrelling, swearing, idleness, pride, and so forth. But the final section of these *Divine Songs* does herald a change. It is called *A Slight Specimen of MORAL Songs*, a title that shows he was aware that he was breaking new ground. The iambics of the psalm tunes give way to anapaests and the tone is almost sprightly. In his preface he recommended that both 'the Language and Measures should be easy, and flowing with Chearfulness', even going so far in the direction of cheerfulness as to suggest that 'the Solemnities of Religion' might be dispensed with so that 'Children might find Delight and Profit together'.[5]

This delight he expressed in pastoral terms, but the profit was still openly didactic.

> Abroad in the Meadows to see the young Lambs
> Run sporting about by the side of their Dams,
>   With Fleeces so clean and so white;
> Or a nest of young Doves in a large open Cage,
> When they play all in Love, without Anger or Rage,
>   How much we may learn from the Sight?[6]

In the same year that *A Song to David* appeared, Charles Wesley published his *Hymns for Children*. In his preface he wrote:

> There are two ways of writing or speaking to children: the one is, to let ourselves down to them: the other, to lift them up to us. Dr Watts has wrote in the former way, and has succeeded admirably well ... The Following hymns are written on the other plan: they contain strong and manly sense ...[7]

Like his brother he probably believed that children should never play and that 'he that plays when he is a boy, will play when he is a man'.[8] Children were to be taught. The overall spirit is not unkindly, yet one could wish that he had not expected little girls to sing

> A female mind and body meet
> And pride and ignorance complete
>   Our total uselessness ...

Like Watts before him, Wesley concludes his book with a section that he calls 'Hymns for the Youngest', and here there is a marked change in tone: a simplicity and tenderness that is typified by the famous 'Gentle Jesus meek and mild'. These very young children, it would seem, are free from sin. They are even identified with the Christ Child himself, and this, together with the Blakean concept of divine guardianship, is one of the dominant themes of these hymns.

The social and theological causes behind such different attitudes towards children are many and complex, but in the field of children's literature one new and irrepressible force that was changing everything was commercialism, and its advent can be dated with some precision, as it was on 18 June 1744 that John Newbery published his first book for children, *A little Pretty Pocket-Book*. The business acumen and publishing genius of Newbery are astounding. At one stroke he created the children's book as we know it: tiny in size, ideal for tiny hands, and with an eye-catching cover. There are pictures, one on almost every page, and a sales gimmick: with every copy went a present – a ball for the boys and a pincushion for the girls.

The preface does tend to be a little austere, but once inside we are in the world of children's games: leap-frog, chuck-farthing, blind man's bluff, and shuttlecock. Each game is illustrated by a little woodcut and, though they may be crude and somewhat lifeless (in their mob-caps and long gowns, knee-length breeches and tricorn hats, the minuscule figures hardly look like children), they were the best to be had at the time. There are Morals and Rules of Life as appendices to each little verse, but they in no way descry the children's sports. The emphasis is everywhere on delight, and, as the title page says, 'Amusement'.

Smart was not only Newbery's son-in-law; he was also, in the early years of his marriage, one of his employees and played his part in this side of the business. He contributed to the *Lilliputian Magazine* and to a number of whimsical anthologies. It was valuable, practical experience in how to write for children, and added to this, after his release from the madhouse, when he was trying to earn a living again, he published *The PARABLES of our LORD and SAVIOUR JESUS CHRIST done into familiar verse with occasional applications for the use and improvement of younger minds*. A writer in the *Critical Review* dismissingly granted that the plain, familiar verse was 'adapted to the capacities of children', but doubted if it would 'please their imaginations, or improve their taste in poetry'.[9] It was fair comment. These parables, written in clumsy octosyllabic couplets, are solemn, unrelieved doggerel, but in writing them Smart did learn something and that was simplicity. The baroque extravagance of *A Song to David* would not do for children, and so, in 1771, when he combined this new simplicity with his own natural lyric gift, the result, his *Hymns for the Amusement of Children* was masterly.

Understandably, whatever working relationship Smart had once had with his father-in-law, it did not survive the break-up of his marriage. It was Merrick's translation of the Psalms that Newbery published, and on his death in 1767 Newbery left a clause in his will to make sure that none of his money ended up in Smart's hands or in those of his creditors. He was quite right in his assumption that Smart would have creditors, and they were beginning to close in. In April 1770 he was arrested for debt. His friends could not or would not bail him out and he was sentenced and confined to the King's Bench Prison. Even this did not totally conquer his high spirits, as we can see from a letter he wrote from prison to his friend Charles Burney.

> Dr Sr
> After being a fortnight in a spunging house, one week in the Marshalsea in the want of all things, I am this day safely arrived at the King's Bench – Seven years in Madhouses, eight times arrested in six years, I beg leave to commend myself to a benevolent and thriving friend.
>
> Yours affectionately,
Christopher Smart.[10]

What help Burney was to give him we do not know, but Thomas Carnan, Smart's brother-in-law, seems not to have shared the view of the rest of his family as he purchased 'The Rules' for him. This meant that Smart was not confined in a cell, but during the daytime was allowed to walk in the fresh air of St George's Fields and within a restricted area around the prison. It was a self-contained little area with shops and a chapel, but some thirty of these shops were gin shops, selling 120 gallons of the stuff between them every week. Bearing in mind Hogarth's *Gin-Lane* and Smart's own drink problem, one would not expect him to survive long in such a place and he did not. Despite the privilege of 'The Rules', he knew real hardship, but, far from being degraded by it, Smart seems to have grown in stature as a Christian. Even when his own personal needs were so great, he again wrote to Burney, this time asking him to help a fellow prisoner, whom he assisted himself 'according to his *willing poverty*'.[11] Charity was one of the lessons Smart set out to teach in his hymns for children and it is clear that he was practising it himself.

It was Thomas Carnan who published *Hymns for the Amusement of Children* in 1771 only a few months before Smart's death, and, although there were at least five editions before the end of the century, and one in America, it is now a very rare book indeed. In the hands of children it would seem to have been so popular that they loved it to destruction.

The great majority of Smart's religious poems are songs of praise and hymns of joy and these are no exception, only the joy is of a different kind. There is no longer the excitement, fervour, and sonorous grandeur of *A Song to David*; instead we have the calm of a secure faith.

With this in mind we can see that the first hymn contains an important introductory statement.

'Faith'

The Father of the Faithful said,
    At God's first calling, 'Here am I;'
Let us by his example sway'd
    Like him submit, like him reply,

'Go take thy son, thine only son,
    'And offer him to God thy King.'
The word was giv'n – the work begun,
    'The altar pile, the victim bring.'

But lo! th' angelic voice above
    Bade the great Patriarch stop his hands;
'Know God is everlasting love,
    'And must revoke such harsh commands.'

Then let us imitate the Seer,
    And tender with compliant grace
Ourselves, our souls, and children here,
    Hereafter in a better place.

(ll. 1–16)

The subject is faith and both poem and woodcut illustrate the story of Abraham and Isaac, a not-unexpected choice for a children's collection, but Smart is more than just a poetic illustrator. He has ideas as well as images, and even the fact that Abraham is never mentioned by name in the poem has a purpose. When he is referred to in the first line as 'The Father of the Faithful', this would have been recognized by a Bible-reading audience as a pointer to St Paul's major writings on faith, either Romans 4: 16, 'the faith of Abraham; who is the father of us all', or Galatians 3: 7, 'Know ye therefore that they which are of the faith, the same are the children of Abraham.' It is against the background of the teaching contained in these epistles that Smart's poem develops the doctrine of justification by faith and the repudiation of the works of the law. Romans 4: 13 reads, 'For the promise, that he should be the heir of the world was not to Abraham, or to his seed, through the law, but through the righteousness of faith.'

It is the stern voice of the Old Testament law that commands Abraham to sacrifice his son – a law both fierce and repressive, the effects of which were still being felt in the eighteenth century, and not least in the harsh demands that were then being made of children. We think of Blake's 'Holy Thursday' in the *Songs of Experience*.

> Is this a holy thing to see
> In a rich and fruitful land –
> Babes reduced to misery,
> Fed with cold usurous hand?
>
> Is that trembling cry a song?
> Can it be a song of joy –
> And so many children poor?
> It is a land of poverty.

In the King's Bench Prison Smart had all around him the victims of this usury and poverty, and his own suffering must have formed and directed his sympathies, yet there is no excess of sympathy, no fashionable sentimentality. At the same time he never directly confronts, or shows any real awareness of the causes of the suffering. Perhaps it is his Christian consciousness of the need to forgive that prevents him from pointing an accusing finger, but there is absolutely no social comment, even on Cowper's level, and his poetry never enters the region of Blakean 'Experience'. Smart could quite possibly have written 'The Lamb', but not 'The Tyger', and certainly not 'London'. Just as in the first little woodcut Isaac is forever spared his father's knife, so in Smart's poetic vision both the violence of reality and the reality of violence are kept at bay. He is above all the poet of innocence.

Innocence can be a positive quality. In the first two stanzas of 'Faith' Smart follows the Bible story closely, but in the third a new element is introduced. In the Bible the angel either relates the word of God, or actually is God (there is some confusion of pronouns in Genesis 22: 12), but in Smart's version it is clear that God and the angel are quite separate. What is more, the angelic voice appears to be rebuking God, saying that His commands are 'harsh' and that he 'must revoke' them. The result is a rebuttal of the law-giving Jehovah and of the darker elements of the Old Testament. Instead, in keeping with his translations of the Psalms, Smart's angel proclaims the doctrine of the evangelicals, 'Know God is everlasting love.' This is the God of the New Testament, who does not expect suffering or a blood sacrifice.

The second Hymn, 'Hope', develops the story of Samuel and Hannah and tells how Hannah had her prayers answered when, after many years of childless marriage, she asked God for a son. Again, this is an appropriate choice for children, but the hymn goes further and has something to say *about* children. Earlier writers of hymns for children, such as Watts and Wesley, had mostly followed Calvin and emphasized the inherent sinfulness of the young, but, as Samuel was dedicated to God even before he was born, so Smart's young readers are taught to sing

> Thus yet a child may I begin
>   To serve the Lord with all my heart;
> To shun the wily lures of sin,
> And claim the prize, or e'er I start.

(ll. 13–16)

Sin, in this context, is something that ensnares children after their birth and so is not inherent but of human origin.

Sin, death, and damnation had been the dominant themes in Watts and Wesley, but so much in Smart is about the joy of being alive; not the threat of damnation but the certainty of salvation.

'For Saturday'

Now's the time for mirth and play,
Saturday's an holyday;
Praise to heav'n unceasing yield,
I've found a lark's nest in the field.

A lark's nest, then your play-mate begs
You'd spare herself and speckled eggs;
Soon she shall ascend and sing
Your praises to th' eternal King.

(ll. 1–8)

What he advocates is benevolence. In 'GOOD-NATURE to Animals' he speaks up for the horses and the dogs and even the silkworms that serve us and so deserve our consideration, but also for the smallest creatures that may do nothing for us but still deserve our love.

Let thine industrious Silk-worms reap
    Their wages to the full,
Nor let neglected Dormice sleep
    To death within thy wool.

Know when the frosty weather comes,
    'Tis charity to deal
To Wren and Redbreast all thy crumbs,
    The remnant of thy meal.

(ll. 13–20)

He knows not everyone will agree with him and that some may think it all too trivial to bother with, but he insists he is right.

Tho' these some spirits think but light,
    And deem indifferent things;
Yet they are serious in the sight
    Of CHRIST, the King of Kings.

(25–8)

And Blake, who knew that 'A robin redbreast in a cage puts all heaven in a rage', would have agreed with him.

Stories from the Bible – Abraham and Isaac, Hannah and Samuel – inform many of these poems, but the *language* of the Bible weaves and interweaves its way throughout. Sometimes it is the basis of an entire poem, as in 'Fortitude', which reworks almost all of Ephesians 6: 10–18, 'Put on the whole armour of God . . .'. But, as in the *Hymns and Spiritual Songs*, readers also need to be alive to Smart's use of the Book of Common Prayer. This is most evident when we come to Hymn XIX and enter upon a sequence that is directly related to Holy Week. It begins with 'Patience', which is the theme of the Collect for the Sunday before Easter and the poems ends with

> Submissive on my bended knee,
> To take my cross and follow Thee.
>
> (ll. 23–4)

The story of Simon of Cyrene carrying Christ's cross is also the Gospel for the day (Matt. 27).

The Gospel for the Monday before Easter contains Christ's words to his disciples 'Watch ye and pray, lest ye enter into temptation' (Mark 14: 38), and this becomes the opening of the second hymn in the sequence, 'Watching'.

> At every tempter's first essay,
> Be sure to watch, be sure to pray;
> For this great requisite the Lord
> Has strongly urg'd upon record.
>
> (ll. 1–4)

This poem also contains a reference to Peter falling asleep and his betrayal of Christ, which are both part of the same gospel reading.

'Generosity' is the hymn for the Tuesday before Easter and it is this which confirms that Smart is following the Book of Common Prayer, as the Gospel for this day is Mark 15, which records the events of the crucifixion itself (it would otherwise look out of order), and stanza three begins:

> The Lord shed on the Holy Rood
> His infinitely gen'rous blood,
> Not for himself, but all . . .
>
> (ll. 13–15)

The title of the fourth poem is 'Gratitude', that single word which is so central to Smart – to his religion, to his poetry, and to his life. 'Generosity' had ended by stating that Christ himself 'is also Gratitude', and in a joyous poem gratitude speaks first as a cherub and then sequentially as all three persons of the Trinity. There is no direct reference to Holy Week in this poem, but the Gospel for the day is Luke 22, the Last Supper, when Christ 'took the cup and gave thanks'.

Hymn XXIII, 'Peace', prays for peace in the Church and this time it is the Epistle for the day, 1 Corinthians 11, that Smart has gone to, where the second verse of the reading is 'For first of all, when ye come together in the church, I hear that there be divisions among you.'

> O come unto the Church repair,
> And her defects review . . .

is Smart's echo of this in a wide-ranging poem.

This brings us to Good Friday and the first lesson for Evensong is from Isaiah 53, where the words 'man of sorrows' also appear in Smart's hymn 'Melancholy'.

'Melancholy' is mostly dark enough for its Good Friday theme, but it is as if gloom is something Smart cannot sustain. The final stanza is already eager for Easter and for the hope of life after death.

> Yet thou didst preach of future bliss,
>   Peace permanent above,
> Of Truth and Mercy's holy kiss,
> Those joys, which none that love thee miss,
>   O give us grace to love.

(ll. 36–40)

After 'Melancholy' comes 'Mirth', which begins

> If you are merry sing away,
>   And touch the organs sweet;
> This is the Lord's triumphant day,
> Ye children in the gall'ries gay,
>   Shout from each goodly seat.

(ll. 1–5)

101

It is an Easter hymn in which the whole world shares in the celebration: the pinks and roses, the cowslips and the lambs. Birds are singing in the hedgerows and the poem ends:

> With white and crimson laughs the sky,
>   With birds the hedge-rows ring;
> To give the praise to God most high,
> And all the sulky fiends defy,
>   Is a most joyful thing.

(ll. 21–5)

Although writing these poems in a debtors' gaol from which he must have known that he was unlikely ever to go free, and perhaps knowing too that he could not have very much longer to live, Smart's joy was in no way diminished, and we find him bringing together here for one last time some of the major themes of his poetry. Joy, praise, and gratitude are everywhere: his own joy in the created world, and that world, by its very existence, praising God and showing in turn its own gratitude.

So many of his beliefs and abilities come together in these poems, but added to them is one simple line, which had been behind everything he had written since the 'Hymn to the Supreme Being' in 1756, and that is the first line of his hymn XVIII, 'Prayer':

Pray without ceasing (says the Saint)

It was his literal acceptance of Paul's command to the Thessalonians, a command that changed his life. As Mrs Thrale explained:

> Smart's melancholy showed itself only in a preternatural excitement to prayer, which he held it as a duty not to controul or repress – *au pied de la lettre* our blessed Saviour's injunction *to pray without ceasing* – so that beginning by regular addresses at stated times to the Almighty, he went on to call his friends from their dinners, or beds, or places of recreation, whenever that impulse towards prayer pressed upon his mind.[12]

It was this that caused him to be locked up, but if we look at the verses on either side of the command in Thessalonians we can see how these verses too determined the shape of so much of the poetry he was to write.

102

16. Rejoice evermore.
17. Pray without ceasing.
18. In every thing give thanks: for this is the will of God in Christ Jesus concerning you.

In spite of the personal disasters this brought him, there is never a moment of regret. The joy and optimism of the man are unwavering. He does not look back, he looks forward and the sequence ends on a note of triumph.

'The CONCLUSION of the Matter'

Fear God – obey his just decrees,
And do it hand, and heart, and knees;
For after all our utmost care
There's nought like penitence and prayer.

Then weigh the balance in your mind,
Look forward, not one glance behind;
Let no foul fiend retard your pace,
Hosanna! Thou hast won the race.

(ll. 1–8)

But in this world Smart himself had won nothing. Through friends at court he had been granted permission to dedicate these hymns to the King's second son, Prince Frederick Augustus, who, although Bishop of Osnabrug, was still only a child of 6 at the time, but, if he had hoped that this might have led to some royal favour and clemency, he was wrong. He died on 20 May 1771, still in the King's Bench Prison, and in a letter to a friend, his nephew, Christopher Hunter, who, twenty years later was to edit a handsome two-volume edition of his uncle's poems, wrote, and with some compassion, 'I trust he is now at peace; it was not his portion here.'[13]

7

An Afterword

Smart's writing career spans little more than twenty-one years, yet within that short space of time the range of his achievement is remarkable. From his secular verse alone one might compile a representative anthology of all that was popular in the first five decades of the eighteenth century. There are fables in the manner of John Gay, an 'Ode on Saint Cecelia's Day', a Georgic, *The Hop-Garden*, which follows the examples of Dyer and Grainger, and *The Hilliad*, a poem that takes its place among a host of other forgotten literary quarrels. Then there are the prologues and epilogues, the epigrams and epitaphs, birthday odes and all sorts of occasional poems about which this study has had little or nothing to say, for if this were all he had written, he would, and not surprisingly, have been forgotten long ago with men like Shenstone and Hurdis. It is only his religious verse that has any significance, yet at the outset even that was equally traditional, equally unremarkable, indeed even somewhat backward-looking.

The blank verse of the Seatonian poems is not a part of that living line that Thomson handed on to Cowper, and that was to reach its peak in Wordsworth's *Prelude*. Sonorous and robust, Smart's blank verse owes everything to Milton. It served a purpose: it brought him sorely needed prize money, early critical attention, and did much to establish his reputation, but it was not going to take him any further. As his fables prove, he could tell a story, but he was not an essayist, and a continuous line of argument was not something he ever managed. He was no Dryden. However, it was all valuable apprenticeship, and in the Seatonian poems one can observe the skills beginning to form, but the finer moments in these poems are moments, and show that essentially he was, as we have seen, a miniaturist. It was a gift he eventually recognized in himself, and in 1760 he wrote in *Jubilate Agno*

> For my talent is to give an impression upon words by punching, that when the reader casts his eye upon 'em, he takes up the image from the mould which I have made.

(B 404)

The very vividness of its image from type founding is itself proof of what he is saying. In writing the single line units of *Jubilate Agno* he was able to hone this gift of *impression*, this precision. Examples are everywhere: 'For all Wrath is Fire, which the adversary blows upon and exasperates' (B 310). So good at it was he that it is all too easy to become acclimatized to *Jubilate Agno*, whereas one ought often to be gasping in astonishment at the daring of this unprecedented verse form.

Smart's greatest gift was as a lyricist, and this is evident in his *Psalms*. What is odd about *The Psalms* is that some progression might be expected throughout the thousands of lines he wrote, some increase in skill with metre and rhyme, but there is none. The reason being that there is no room for progression. This is a verse form in which he was instantly at ease from the start.

There is poetry of a very high order in his psalms, but it is perhaps inevitable that they will always tend to be regarded as the training ground for that unsurpassed lyric *A Song to David*. His psalms were versions rather than translations, but Smart never allowed himself the kinds of freedom that Watts took; he never, for example, followed Watts's boldness with half-rhyme. His versions were much more traditional. But *A Song to David* gave him for the first time the total freedom to compose a religious lyric of his own, and what he did was to bring back some of the grandiloquence of the Seatonian poems. Yet he himself suggested that the poem's 'exact Regularity and Method' was its 'chief fault' (*PW* ii. 117). But he was perhaps not being totally serious. It is ironic that one of the most methodical features of the poem – the rising and falling through twenty-one stanzas of the word ADORATION – is also one of the poem's chief glories. With this in mind, the best word to describe *A Song to David* might be *baroque*. It is like

105

Vivaldi: sensual, exuberant, and grandiose, but also rhetorical in the true sense of the word, and mathematically exact.

This exactness is equally evident in the *Hymns*, as Smart creates a poetical calendar of the church year with precise allusions to and echoes of the Book of Common Prayer. It is still sensuous and there is still exuberance, but overall it is a calmer work than the *Song*. Calm is followed by simplicity – learned through the *Parables* – and then given to us with such a charge of electrical spirituality in the *Hymns for the Amusement of Children* that we cannot help but think of Blake. And so a career that began by looking backwards ends by showing us the future.

The evidence that Blake had read Smart's *Hymns for the Amusement of Children* and perhaps even knew of *Jubilate Agno* is stronger than circumstantial. The link is there in William Cowper and William Hayley. Cowper had subscribed to Smart's *Poems on Several Occasions* (1752), and to *The Psalms*, and Charles Ryskamp, in his biographical study of Cowper's early years, provides evidence that the two poets were acquainted with each other, even if not close friends. They certainly had friends in common. Spencer Madan, Cowper's cousin, had acted in Smart's play *A Trip to Cambridge*, and Bonnel Thornton, a lifelong friend of Smart's, was one of 'the three persons with whom Mr Cowper was most intimate, when he resided in the Temple'.[1] And Ryskamp concludes, 'There were many associations which would lead one to suppose that Cowper and Smart were known to each other'.[2]

The link between the two men and the texts is full of irony, for just when Smart was being released from his madhouse, so it was being decided that the time had come to shut Cowper up in St Albans. Wiliam Hayley, a distinguished poet in his day, who was to be Cowper's first biographer, supported him we are told, 'at a time when his mania was beyond the comprehension of even his most enlightened contemporaries',[3] and his affliction and a possible cure for it were the subject of much discussion and correspondence between Hayley and the Revd Thomas Cawardine. Somehow the manuscript of *Jubilate Agno* came into their hands, and as W. H. Bond says, 'was regarded by them as a kind of case study in poetic mania'.[4]

Hayley was later to become a friend and patron of Blake, and Blake went to live nearby him in a cottage in Felpham in

1800, the year of Cowper's death. It was then that Hayley decided to write the biography and he commissioned Blake to engrave a portrait of Cowper. Peter Ackroyd suggests, 'he must have been of interest to Blake, who had himself suffered from the imputation of insanity and even religious mania ... He [Blake] must have discussed Cowper with Hayley, even as he worked upon his visage, and he became acquainted with some of those who had known Cowper well.'[5] That *Jubilate Agno* featured in their conversation is, at the very least, highly probable, and it is also probable that Blake knew of the *Hymns for the Amusement of Children*. This is not to suggest any influence of Smart on Blake; the dates of the *Songs of Innocence and Experience* would be likely to preclude that, but to be able to link these two 'eccentric' poets in this way is to put one more nail into the coffin of uniqueness.

Blake is one of our foremost religious poets, yet he was rarely, if ever, a church-goer, and the same seems to be true of Smart, who favoured praying out of doors.

> For I prophecy that the praise of God will be in every man's mouth in the Publick streets.
> For I prophecy that there will be Publick worship in the cross ways and fields.

(JA C 62–3)

He also preferred prayer to be loud.

> For the AIR is purified by prayer which is made aloud and with all our might.

(JA B 224)

Small wonder that he routed all the company in St James's Park.

It is clear from *Jubilate Agno* that he was, nevertheless, an Anglican and that his Anglicanism was important to him, but his religious standpoint is not simple enough to label. He was bitterly hostile to the Church of Rome, yet we find him praying 'Let Mary rejoice with the Maid – blessed be the name of the immaculate CONCEPTION' (B 139), which is a decidedly Roman doctrine. He held an extreme view of the Church of England's position in the world. 'For I bless God that the CHURCH of ENGLAND is one of the SEVEN ev'n the candlestick of the Lord'

107

(B 126), whereas the seven churches so symbolized in Revelation 1: 20 were all in what is now Turkey. Even this did not satisfy Smart; he wanted and expected the Church of England to be 'the head of Europe in the spirit' (*JA* C 102). At the same time he also saw the need for reform in the Church, especially of the liturgy (B 252).

One of the strongest elements of Smart's religion was his love of the created world. Devlin has called it 'Franciscan', adding, 'The adjective Franciscan is sometimes used in a way that has no relation to the actual life and history of St Francis of Assisi. But in this case there is at least a *prima facie* resemblance – poverty, humiliation and suffering accepted without rancour and even with a kind of joy'.[6] Rancour there was not. Equally as strong as his love for the world was his love for his fellow men, his benevolence, his charity, and 'good-nature'. As early as 1752 he published a poem 'On Good-Nature', which shows that in his view this was not simply some sort of passive, docile, 'inoffensive' sort of quality, but the very essence of an active virtue; it is, he says, what turns *existence* into *life*.

It should not surprise us that the Age of Reason was also an Age of Feeling. 'Use all the passions!' Smart had commanded in *A Song to David* (l. 259), and in this he was a part of that conscious revolt against the mistrust of passions and the exaggerated claims made for stoic rationality that was now being heard in sermon after sermon.

> Our Reason has but little to do in the forming of our minds, and bringing us to a vertuous Religious Life; 'tis our Passions and Affections that must do the work, for till they begin to move, our Reason is but like a chariot when the Wheels are off, that is never like to perform the journey.[7]

Smart made that journey. In direct opposition to the Calvinistic belief in the depravity of man, voices were beginning to argue for a more optimistic appraisal of human nature, and among them Smart's voice was one of the most eloquent. His faith and his optimism were irrepressible. Even on release from the madhouse, when all his hopes were dashed and he had to face up to disappointment and loneliness and to the failure of his greatest poem, he was still able to write, in that same year, in his 'Ode on a Bed of Guernsey Lilies', a line so moving in its simplicity that one could wish it for him as an epitaph: 'We never are deserted quite.'

'On a Bed of Guernsey Lilies'
Written in September 1763.

Ye beauties! O how great the sum
   Of sweetness that ye bring;
On what a charity ye come
   To bless the latter spring!
How kind the visit that ye pay,
Like strangers on a rainy day,
   When heartiness despair'd of guests:
No neighbour's praise your pride alarms,
No rival flow'r surveys your charms,
   Or heightens, or contests!

Lo, thro' her works gay nature grieves
   How brief she is and frail,
As ever o'er the falling leaves
   Autumnal winds prevail.
Yet still the philosophic mind
Consolatory food can find,
   And hope her anchorage maintain:
We never are deserted quite;
   'Tis by succession of delight
That love supports his reign.

Notes

CHAPTER 1. 'HYMN TO THE SUPREME BEING' AND THE SEATONIAN POEMS

1. Arthur Sherbo, *Christopher Smart: Scholar of the University* (East Lancing, Mich., 1967), 106. Oliver Goldsmith was less fortunate: he fell ill, sent out for Dr James's Fever Powders, took them, and died.
2. Ibid. 113.
3. *Correspondence of Thomas Gray*, ed. P. Toynbee and L. Whibley (Oxford, 1935), 273.
4. Ibid. 291.
5. *Boswell's Life of Johnson*, ed. G. B. Hill (Oxford, 1934), i. 397.
6. Sherbo, *Christopher Smart*, 127.
7. *Boswell's Life of Johnson*, 397.
8. E. G. Ainsworth and C. E. Noyes, *Christopher Smart: A Biographical and Critical Study* (University of Missouri Studies, 18/4; Columbia, 1943), 82.
9. *Monthly Review*, 7 (1752), 131.
10. Ibid. 4 (1751), 508.
11. Ibid. 7 (1752), 131.
12. Ainsworth and Noyes, *Christopher Smart*, 81.
13. *Gentleman's Magazine*, 25 (1754), 93.
14. Christopher Devlin, *Poor Kit Smart* (London, 1961), 73.
15. *Monthly Review*, 14 (1756), 554–7.
16. Sherbo, *Christopher Smart*, 119.
17. *Monthly Review*, 28 (1758), 321.

CHAPTER 2. *JUBILATE AGNO*

1. Arthur Sherbo, 'The Dating and Order of the Fragments of Christopher Smart's *Jubilate Agno'*, *Harvard Library Bulletin*, 10 (1956), 201–7.

2. *Boswell's Life of Johnson*, ed. G. B. Hill (Oxford, 1934), i. 397.
3. W. H. Bond, 'Introduction', in *Jubilate Agno*, ed. W. H. Bond (London, 1954), 17.
4. Arthur Sherbo, *Christopher Smart: Scholar of the University* (East Lancing, Mich., 1967), 106.
5. Robert Lowth, *Lectures on the Sacred Poetry of the Hebrews*, trans. G. Gregory (London, 1816), i. 25.
6. Ibid. 100.
7. For examples of amplification, see B 125; for accumulation, B 46–8; for apposition, B 112.
8. Lowth, *Lectures*, 56.
9. See 'Hymn XXVII', in *Hymns for the Amusement of Children*.
10. D. J. Greene, 'Smart, Berkeley, the Scientists and the Poets', *JHI* 14 (1953), 327–52.
11. Karina Williamson, 'Smart's *Principia*: Science and Anti-Science in *Jubilate Agno*', *Review of English Studies*, 30 (1979), 409–22.
12. I am indebted to Dr Andy Amos for his advice and assistance on scientific matters in this chapter.
13. Bond, 'Introduction', 21.
14. Ibid. 23.
15. Arthur Sherbo, 'Christopher Smart, Reader of Obituaries', *MLN* 71 (1956), 117–82.
16. Christopher Devlin, *Poor Kit Smart* (London, 1961), 133.

CHAPTER 3. *THE PSALMS OF DAVID*

1. All quotations from the Psalms are taken from the Book of Common Prayer, which is the version Smart worked from.
2. Christopher Hunter, 'Introduction', in *The Poems of the Late Christopher Smart*, ed. Christopher Hunter (Reading, 1791), i, p. xxviii.
3. Maynard Mack, *Alexander Pope: A Life* (London, 1985), 564.
4. Yet it has been calculated that between 1414 and 1862 there were 263 complete versions of the Psalter. See Daniel Sedwick, *A Comprehensive Index of the Names of Original Authors of Hymns, Versifiers of Psalms, and Translators from Several Languages* (London, 1863).
5. C. S. Phillips, *Hymnody Past and Present* (London, 1937), 143.
6. John Dryden, 'Preface' to *Aeneis*, in *Of Dramatic Poetry* (Everyman edn.; London, 1962), ii. 247.
7. Isaac Watts, *Works* (Leeds, 1800), i, p. xlv.
8. Charles Ryskamp, *William Cowper of the Inner Temple, Esquire* (Cambridge, 1959), 94.

9. Christopher Devlin, *Poor Kit Smart* (London, 1961), 170.
10. *Monthly Review*, 33 (1763), 240–1.
11. *Critical Review*, 20 (1763), 210–11.
12. James Merrick, *The Psalms, Translated or Paraphrased into English Verse* (Reading, 1763), Psalm 38: 57–60.
13. Hunter, 'Introduction', p. xliii.
14. Elizabeth Anne Smart Le Noir, *Miscellaneous Poems*, (1826), ii. 71.

CHAPTER 4. *A SONG TO DAVID*

1. *Monthly Review*, 28 (1763), 321.
2. *Critical Review*, 25 (1763), 324.
3. Arthur Sherbo, *Christopher Smart: Scholar of the University* (East Lancing, Mich., 1967), 186–7.
4. *Monthly Review*, 29 (1763), 398.
5. Critical Review, 26 (1763), 395.
6. Elizabeth Anne Smart Le Noir, *Miscellaneous Poems* (Reading, 1826), ii. 71.
7. J. Churton Collins, *Treasury of Minor British Poetry* (London, 1896), 395.
8. Robert Brittain, 'An Early Model for *A Song to David*', PMLA 56 (1941), 165–74.
9. Northrop Frye, *Fables of Identity* (New York, 1963), 137.
10. Sherbo, *Christopher Smart*, 172.
11. Patrick Delany, *An Historical Account of the Life and Reign of David King of Israel* (London, 1740–2), i. 241.
12. Ibid. 327.
13. Ibid. 135.
14. Sherbo, *Christopher Smart*, 174.
15. Delany, *An Historical Account*, 186–9.
16. A. G. Mackey, *Lexicon of Freemasonry* (London, 1861), 301.
17. Robert Lowth, *Lectures on the Sacred Poetry of the Hebrews*, trans. G. Gregory (London, 1816), i. 346–7.
18. Christopher Devlin, *Poor Kit Smart* (London, 1961), 141.
19. Francis D. Adams, 'The Seven Pillars of Christopher Smart', *Papers in English Language and Literature*, 1 (1965), 125–32.
20. Ibid. 130.
21. K. M Rogers, 'The Pillars of the Lord: Some Sources of "A Song to David"', *Philological Quarterly*, 40 (1961), 525–34.
22. Moira Dearnley, *The Poetry of Christopher Smart* (London, 1968), 184.
23. *Monthly Review*, 29 (1763), 321.

24. The word was not recorded by Johnson, who says in his Dictionary that no words in our language begin with X.

CHAPTER 5. *HYMNS AND SPIRITUAL SONGS*

1. *Jonathan Swift*, ed. Herbert Davis (Oxford, 1939), ix. 329.
2. Samuel Johnson, *Lives of the English Poets*, ed. G. B. Hill (Oxford, 1905), ii. 310.
3. F. J. Gillman, *The Evolution of the English Hymn* (London, 1927), 135.
4. George Eliot, *Scenes from Clerical Life*, ed. Thomas A. Noble (London, 1985), 8.
5. Scott Elledge (ed.), *Eighteenth Century Critical Essays* (Cornell, 1961), i. 150.
6. Moira Dearnley, *The Poetry of Christopher Smart* (London, 1968), 249–63.
7. Ibid. 250.
8. The celebration of these Solemn Days was discontinued in the nineteenth century.
9. Maynard Mack, *Alexander Pope: A Life* (London, 1985), 9.
10. *Monthly Review*, 31 (1763), 231.
11. *Critical Review*, 15 (1763), 325.
12. Isaac Watts, *The Works* (Leeds, 1800), bk. II, no. 10.
13. Ibid., bk. II, no. 48.
14. Ibid., bk. II, no.18.
15. Christopher Hunter, 'Introduction', in *The Poems of the Late Christopher Smart*, ed. Christopher Hunter (Reading, 1791), i. xxviii.

CHAPTER 6. *HYMNS FOR THE AMUSEMENT OF CHILDREN*

1. Paul Sangster, *Pity My Simplicity* (London, 1963), 30.
2. Issac Watts, 'Obedience to Parents', in *Divine Songs Attempted in Easy Language for the Use of Children* (London, 1715; 1776 edn.), ll. 5–12.
3. Preface to ibid., p. viii.
4. 'Song X', in ibid., ll. 13–16.
5. Ibid. 43.
6. 'Innocent Play', in ibid., ll. 1–6.
7. Sangster, *Pity My Simplicity*, 44.

8. Ibid. 100.
9. *The Poetical Works of Christopher Smart*, ed. Marcus Walsh and Karina Williamson, 5 vols. (Oxford, 1980–96), ii. 201.
10. *The Annotated Letters of Christopher Smart*, ed. Betty Rizzo and Robert Mahony (Carbondale, Ill.: Southern Illinois University Press, 1991), 132.
11. *The Early Diary of Frances Burney*, ed. Annie Raine Ellis (London, 1889), i. 127.
12. *Thraliana, The Diary of Mrs Hester Lynch Thrale (Later Mrs Piozzi) 1776–1809*, ed. Katherine C. Balderston (Oxford, 1942), ii. 728.
13. Arthur Sherbo, *Christopher Smart: Scholar of the University* (East Lancing, Mich., 1967), 265.

CHAPTER 7. AN AFTERWORD

1. Newton to Hannah Moore, quoted Charles Ryskamp, *William Cowper of the Inner Temple, Esquire* (Cambridge, 1959), 79.
2. Ibid. 94.
3. Peter Ackroyd, *Blake* (London, 1995), 215.
4. W. H. Bond, 'Introduction', in *Jubilate Agno*, ed. W. H. Bond (London, 1954), ed. W. H. Bond, 16–17.
5. Ackroyd, 222–3.
6. Christopher Devlin, *Poor Kit Smart* (London, 1961), 17.
7. Charles Hickman, Bishop of Derry; quoted by R. S. Crane in 'Suggestions towards a Genealogy of the "Man of Feeling" ', in Kathleen Williams (ed.), *Backgrounds to Eighteenth Century Literature* (Scranton, Pa., 1971), 331.

Select Bibliography

EDITIONS

Christopher Smart: The Collected Poems, ed. Norman Callan, 2 vols. (London, 1949). Long out of print, which is a pity, as it is a very convenient and clearly set-out collected edition, although it does print *Jubilate Agno* in what later came to be recognized as the wrong way.

Christopher Smart: Jubilate Agno, ed. W. H. Bond (London, 1954). This is the pioneering edition of *Jubilate Agno*, which established the correct way in which it should be read. Its explanatory footnotes are fascinating and show the extent of Smart's eccentric knowledge.

The Poetical Works of Christopher Smart, ed. Marcus Walsh and Karina Williamson, 5 vols. (Oxford, 1980–96). This is the authoritative edition of Smart and is excellent in every respect, but inevitably it is very expensive.

Christopher Smart: Selected Poems, ed. Karina Williamson and Marcus Walsh (London, 1990). This is the Penguin edition and offers a splendid selection of almost every aspect of Smart's work. It seems a pity that more space was not allowed for a thorough introduction and that the notes are rather limited and poorly presented.

The Annotated Letters of Christopher Smart, ed. Betty Rizzo and Robert Mahony (Carbondale, Ill.: Southern Illinois University Press, 1991).

BIBLIOGRAPHY

Mahony, Robert, and Rizzo, Betty W., *Christopher Smart: An Annotated Bibliography, 1743–1983* (New York, 1984).

BIOGRAPHY

Ainsworth, E. G., and Noyes, C. E., *Christopher Smart: A Biographical and Critical Study* (University of Missouri Studies, 18/4; Columbia, 1943). Out of print and difficult to obtain, but it is a fine book and it lay the groundwork for most of the studies that followed.

Devlin, Christopher, *Poor Kit Smart* (London, 1961). A brilliant book. It covers so much ground so briefly and so clearly. It deals with both

115

Smart's life and his poetry. It is an example of how criticism should be written.

Sherbo, Arthur, *Christopher Smart: Scholar of the University* (East Lancing, Mich., 1967). A work of exemplary scholarship, the result of a lifetime's painstaking research, yet it is clear that he never stopped loving his subject.

CRITICISM

Anderson, Frances E., *Christopher Smart* (New York, 1974). A straightforward if rather pedestrian introduction to Smart's life and work.

Blaydes, Sophia B., *Christopher Smart as a Poet of his Time* (The Hague, 1966). Contains much useful background information and an extensive study of *A Song of David*.

Davie, Donald, 'Christopher Smart: Some Neglected Poems', *Eighteenth-Century Studies*, 3 (1970), 242–64. Provides a valuable insight into Smart's Psalms and Hymns.

England, Martha Winburn, and Sparrow, John, *Hymns Unbidden* (New York, 1966). A close look at eighteenth-century hymns, including those of Watts and Wesley.

Dearnley, Moira, *The Poetry of Christopher Smart* (London, 1968). This is an authoritative work without ever being pedantic. It also covers the secular poems.

Greene, D. J., 'Smart, Berkeley, the Scientists and the Poets', *Journal of the History of Ideas*, 14 (1953), 327–52. A study of Smart's thinking and of the scientific ideas of his day.

Grigson, Geoffrey, *Christopher Smart* (London, 1961). A fine brief study by a perceptive critic.

Guest, Harriet, *A Form of Sound Words: The Religious Poetry of Christopher Smart* (Oxford, 1989). A scholarly and academic work written for scholars and academics.

Hartman, Geoffrey H., 'Christopher Smart's "Magnificat": Towards a Theory of Representation', in *The Fate of Reading* (Chicago, 1975).

Hawes, Clement, *Mania and Literary Style: The Rhetoric of Enthusiasm from the Ranters to Christopher Smart* (Cambridge, 1996). A specialist approach to a somewhat limited area of study, but raises some interesting issues.

—— (ed.), *Christopher Smart and the Enlightenment* (New York, 1999). A varied collection of academic studies.

Kuhn, A. J., 'Christopher Smart: The Poet as Patriot of the Lord, *ELH* 30 (1963), 121–36.

Spacks, Patricia Meyer, *The Poetry of Vision: Five Eighteenth-Century Poets* (Cambridge, Mass., 1967). An anthology with a useful introduction that relates Smart to the other poets of his day.

Williamson, Karina, 'Smart's *Principia*: Science and Anti-Science in *Jubilate Agno*', *Review of English Studies*, 30 (1979), 409–22. A fine study of Smart's scientific thinking.

Index

Printed and bound by CPI Group (UK) Ltd, Croydon, CR0 4YY

13/04/2025

14656586-0004